CW01334916

THE
BITCOIN-DOLLAR

THE
BITCOIN-DOLLAR

Mark Goodwin

Bitcoin Magazine Books
Nashville, TN

The Bitcoin-Dollar by Mark Goodwin
© 2023 by Mark Goodwin, all rights reserved. No portion of this book may be reproduced, distributed, or transmitted in whole or part without written permission of the publishers. Please maintain author and publisher information, including this page and metadata, with any reproduction, distribution, or transmission, in whole or in part.

Portions of this content were originally published in *Bitcoin Magazine*.

ISBN 979-8-9876363-3-6 – (paperback)
ISBN 979-8-9876363-4-3 – (ebook)

≋‖ BITCOIN MAGAZINE BOOKS

Published by Bitcoin Magazine Books
An imprint of BTC Media, LLC
438 Houston St. #257 Nashville, TN 37203

Address all inquiries to contact@btcmedia.org

Cover design by Annabelle Bazi

Interior design by MediaNeighbours.com

The views and conclusions expressed in this manuscript are entirely the author's own and do not necessarily reflect those of BTC Media, LLC or its employees, agents, partners, and associates.

Bitcoin Magazine Books is a trademark of BTC Media, LLC, all rights reserved, and may not be reproduced without written permission of the publisher.

for my parents

Contents

Introduction: An Economic Monomyth............1

Part I - The Bitcoin-Dollar.................................3
Chapter 1: The Birth of the Bitcoin-Dollar................5
Chapter 2: The Stablecoin Monster 23
Chapter 3: Castles Made of Sand Dollars 33
Chapter 4: The Nakamoto Accord 53
Chapter 5: Ideal Banking...71
Chapter 6: The Nashian Orientation 87

Part II - The Fight for Bitcoin 99
Chapter 7: Water's Warm Maximalism 101
Chapter 8: Us and Them 111
Chapter 9: The Lightning Round.......................... 123
Chapter 10: There Is No Political Solution............. 135
Chapter 11: Space, Energy, and Time.......................155
Chapter 12: Life After Issuance 179
Conclusion: A Means To An End..........................189
Glossary 197
Acknowledgments 207
About the Author.. 209

Introduction

An Economic Monomyth

Money is a technological tool that communicates settlement between parties. The ultimate goal of money is to transmit trust within context, typically over time and over space. The distinction of the need for value settlement between time and space has allowed for a separation between commodity and currency. The dollar has arguably been the closest we have seen to succeeding at both of these tasks until the launch of Bitcoin at the start of 2009. The transitional period we are about to experience is simply the current iteration of an eternal concept of humans and money – an economic monomyth. If this book could have been written without using the words dollar or bitcoin, it would have. Yet an economic system that grows and regulates itself purely by the actions of its participants and not its rulers is a distortion of the status quo. Bitcoin is a state change of money, settlement, and economic policy that takes us out from underneath the poles of the currency and commodity dichotomy.

Mark Goodwin
August, 2023

PART ONE

THE BITCOIN-DOLLAR

⋞ One ⋟

The Birth of the Bitcoin-Dollar

You have probably heard of the petrodollar. You may not know the ins and outs, but you have heard the term in history class or on some podcast. In a very simple and reductive way, it is an abstract noun meant to show the political and military denomination of the US dollar as the sole purchasing currency of oil. By creating the exclusive medium of exchange to be their dollar, be it in treasuries, bonds or cash, the United States could "quantitatively ease" their expanding monetary supply into the ever-demanded energy commodity that is oil.

The idea of tying your monetary system to an energy system might seem a bit odd at first but consider the actual exchange of capital to be one of time spent earning the pay (working debt for credit capital) for a direct-product-of or service-based expression of the seller's time. It might seem trite, but time is money – perhaps the most accurate commodity of the free market. So, by tying your hard-earned greenbacks to an energy-derived system, one can help preserve the scarcity of time spent earning.

This is the concept behind the numerous bimetallic standards the United States has applied before, during and after the revolution of 1776. One central bank and 195 years later, Richard Nixon closed the gold window, severing the stable tie of the dollar to the price of gold, and escorted us into the wide and open skies of fiat currency. What felt like high flying through the following decades was actually falling deeper and deeper into the cavernous hole of an ever-expanding debt balloon. Monetary growth expanded from $636 billion in January 1971 to an absurd $7.4 trillion by the time our fiat experiment caught up to us in the winter of 2007. The pressures of the cascading defaults of a Frankenstein financial creation hit in 2008; a monstrous body of illicit subprime mortgage speculation with the head of a eurodollar system liquidity squeeze.

By the time the news broke of a single hedge fund in the EU defaulting, the fears of insolvency in the system ran as far as New York City. In September 2008, a bank run at the fractionally reserved Lehman Brothers drained the 161-year-old institution in a single afternoon. Why would issues with the credit of a single firm cause a global recession? Why would a bad trade for a hedge fund have this much effect on the United States dollar system, never mind the rest of the world's currencies? The answers are concurrently abstract when identifying an exact psychological cause, for, after all, money is just a communications tool, but shockingly simple in an economic sense. Every market of every kind can be reduced to simple supply and demand. At the fundamental core, every market consists of buyers and sellers. So how did this assumed localized liquidity crisis from a hedge fund default suddenly become a global problem?

Not only did they not have the money to pay the debt in liquid reserves in the bank when the chickens came to roost, but they had already sold packaged shares of their debt around the global financial market. Large hedge funds happily bought these compartmentalized debts in order to allow portions of their wealth to earn interest in the form of another firm's debt. It was a nice gambit for a while; the smaller, less liquid companies got access to much-needed credit, and the larger, more established companies got to earn slim but compounding percentages on assumed future profits. Everyone's a winner, baby. But when one of those small debtors goes under, like in the case of the narrative of a local default due to some poor and over-leveraged mortgage plays, the larger firms are caught holding the realized loss of their now defaulted debt purchases; overnight that cheap and easy debt became very expensive.

But these days of wine-and-roses Ponzi of repackaged, fractionalized debt-for-credit-now was not just enjoyed by a small chain of firms but nearly the entire financial system. The once healthy and strong tree was now a rotten log, eaten away from the inside by vicious, parasitic debtors and gluttonous, grubby creditors. A system-wide dollar liquidity crunch led to defaults and bank runs which simultaneously led to a system-wide dollar liquidity crunch. A financial crisis perfectly placed right between a Red and Blue president should sound awfully familiar.

But in 2007, there was Ben Bernanke, nominated by George W. Bush and later renominated by Barack Obama, to bail out the banking system that just got caught with their pants down. After gambling with homeowner's debt via fractional reserve margin plays, the American banking system turned to the lender of last resort, the Federal Reserve and the Treasury, to generate liquidity by printing dollars. The future money printing savant Steven Mnuchin, then of OneWest Bank, profiteered on the bailouts, collecting massive service fees and executive bonuses for the very people and corporations that caused (see: benefited from) the recession in the first place. As the working class licked their wounds and prepared for winter, the Cantillonaires feasted on an eroded housing market and cheap index funds.

We have seen practically nothing but unmitigated growth in markets since these purple bailouts, which really only stood to further drive wealth inequality in the coming decade (further exacerbated by the lockdowns). The once unifying financial protests slowly faded into a divided, bipartisan culture clash, with the liberals blaming the Bush administration and the conservatives blaming Obama's. In a sign of mutual-assured profits, when given the opportunity to prosecute Mnuchin of aforementioned fraud, then acting

DA of California and now Vice President Kamala Harris declined to press any charges whatsoever, and, in fact, he later became the Secretary of the Treasury a decade later under President Trump.

So we can see how the violent monetary base expansion of the United States dollar could inflate away the purchasing power of an individual dollar, hurting savers and those with dollar-denominated positions, but why did this not hurt the United States' purchasing power on a net basis? Why didn't the massive inflation of dollars, from well under $1 trillion in 1971 to $10 trillion in 2012, bring the economy to its knees and relinquish economic reserve hegemony to China or Japan (our biggest debtors)? By the time millions of Americans found themselves without homes and the Occupy Wall Street movement fizzled out, the Federal Reserve was back to business as usual, raising interest rates and resuming sales of bonds to foreign entities (and eventually to itself). How were we able to fight off the mechanics of an unhinged money supply decreasing its demand?

The reality is that the United States never left an energy standard – we just simply switched from a gold-backed dollar system to an oil-based dollar system. With the decree of 1971, the gold dollar was destroyed, and in its place, the petrodollar was born. American Imperialism has worn many clothes, red and blue cloth alike, but it has always been for one purpose; to make more money. The activity in the Middle East, starting with the Marines landing in Beirut in 1958, mutated into a proxy war in Afghanistan between the USSR and the US during the Cold War, and finally grew into a full-scale occupation in the summer of 1990 with Bush Senior's directed invasion of Kuwait.

By occupying the oil-rich nations of the region, the United States enforced the sole denomination of the market share of all petrol sales to foreign entities in dollars. This allowed the Fed to expand our monetary supply, slowly but surely over 50 years, with no apparent loss of demand. Oil-dependent countries across Eurasia were forced to buy dollars before purchasing the precious petrol needed to power their industrial expansion. By 1990, the US dollar system had expanded to $3 trillion. Over the next 30 years, the United States had spread its power with maneuvers in Iraq, Syria, Lebanon, Yemen, Turkey, Jordan, Saudi Arabia and only now are we removing the last remaining military presence in Afghanistan; by the fall of 2021, the US dollar system stood at $20 trillion.

So, why did we move our military presence out of the region then? Seems like an inappropriate lever to give up in a time when inflation has been acknowledged by retail and a pandemic disrupts supply chains and labor forces across the globe. Why would we want to jeopardize our world currency reserve status by removing our ability to prop up the dollar's demand, as global interest rates sat at zero (or even below?) A Ponzi cannot simply be tapered, and we continually find ourselves mere weeks away from smacking into our debt ceiling and risking default.

Historically, the United States has raised the debt ceiling countless times in recent memory across all expressions of political spectrum in the three branches of government, and such are trained to expect the same. We have always had a place to put that newfound supply of debt expansion into the forced demands of a petrol-based dollar system. What makes this threat of default perhaps different from the 2008 crisis? It is nearly the same setup, with a diversified, debt-riddled real estate market on the brink of defaulting, with China's Evergrande auditioning for the role of the Lehman Brothers, causing a short-term deflationary pressure on the global dollar system. We know more printing is going to come to prevent the default of China's real estate market, as well as prevent the US from defaulting on its loans.

But it isn't quite the same for a mathematically succinct reason; the compounding service of our nearly $33 trillion dollars of debt is now beyond the growth of the GDP of the country. We cannot simply raise interest rates forever due to this debt service, and yet with the acknowledgment of inflation running far beyond the targeted 2% per year, the once formidable long-term treasury bond yields have made the $120 trillion dollar-denominated bond market mathematically worthless. If a bank bought a large amount of 10-year bonds expecting a yield of 2% over a decade, their money is now stuck, no longer generating any profits. The not-yet matured bonds went from guaranteed profits to not even keeping up with the inflationary action of the dollar in just the first year.

The last time we saw the markets on the ropes was March 2020; oil futures went negative, bitcoin halved in value, and precious metals and stock indexes across the economy hemorrhaged value simultaneously. If you were lucky enough to have supplied yourself with the knowledge, it was a once-in-a-generational buying opportunity for commodities. A mere two months later, Bitcoin nodes across the globe enforced the third of 32 supply issuance halvings and decreased the block reward from 12.5 BTC to 6.25 BTC per mined block. For the first time ever, the relative bitcoin supply issuance was below 2%, and thus below the average inflation of both gold coming out of the ground and the average inflation of the United States dollar. By that same time next year, bitcoin had run from just above $3,200 to nearly $65,000. There were very few aware of it at the time, but on that dark Thursday back in March, a new financial instrument was born: the bitcoin-dollar.

Satoshi Nakamoto's Bitcoin was directly inspired by the events of 2008, immortalizing *The Times*' headline from January 9, 2009, in its inaugural genesis block. Today, we find ourselves again on the brink of another bailout. A signaling by the Fed on their dot chart of tapering off bond purchases causes market retraction, and an explanation the next day by a Fed chair causes dovish reclaims of yesterday's all-time highs. If we raise interest rates, we can no longer afford our debt service, and if we don't raise interest rates, we allow further debt expansion, monetary debasement and loss of purchasing power of the net dollar system. How can we continue to keep up demand for the dollar while still pumping the money supply to pay off our compounding debts? In retrospect, it was inevitable that the first country to adopt bitcoin would be dollarized. El Salvador, the first nation-state to adopt bitcoin as legal tender, is one of 66 dollarized countries in the world. Nearly 70% of the population remains unbanked and almost a quarter of their GDP is created via USD-denominated remittance payments. Native to the execution of their Chivo wallet, a Lightning-enabled app based on Jack Maller's Strike, is the use of a stablecoin pegged to the dollar. In fact, in a few regions, Strike directly uses the oft-misunderstood Tether, or USDT: the largest stablecoin by market cap at nearly $70 billion.

Why does this matter? Aren't customers simply using the dollar stablecoin for a moment before transferring and storing their value onto the Bitcoin network? By creating an infrastructural on-ramp to Satoshi's protocol that is denominated in dollars, we have in effect recreated the same ever-present demand for an inflating supply of dollars demonstrated in the petrodollar system. This does not mean you cannot use euros or pounds to purchase bitcoin, just like there was never a literal monopoly on the sale of oil in dollars, but the volume on BTC trading pairs is arguably inconsequential outside of dollar-denominated markets; BTC/USD pairs make up the vast majority of volume on the global market. By expanding the Tether market cap to $68.7 billion during the first dozen or so years of Bitcoin's life, when 83% of total supply was issued, the US market made sure the value being imbued into the now-disinflationary protocol would forever be symbiotically related to the dollar system.

Tether isn't simply "tethering" the dollar to bitcoin but permanently linking the new global, permissionless energy market to the United States' monetary policy. We have recreated the petrodollar mechanisms that allow retention of net-purchasing power for the US economy despite monetary base expansion. If the peg of a dollar-denominated stablecoin falls below one-to-one, large arbitrage opportunities are created for investors, bankers and nation-states to acquire dollar-strength purchasing power for 99 cents on the dollar. This occurs when expanding stablecoin supply leads to less demand, and those trying to purchase dollar-denominated commodities on bitcoin/USD pairs are forced to sell at a slight perceived loss. So, like any market, when supply increases cause demand to decrease, the selling price moves down; the selling price moving down briefly below a dollar causes demand to increase and suddenly we are repegged at 1:1.

The reason this works uniquely with bitcoin versus oil or gold is the verifiable, auditable and scarce monetary policy of the Nakamoto Consensus; there will never even be 21 million bitcoin. By combining a decentralized timestamp server via proof-of-work to solve the digital double-spend problem with a hard-capped token distribution innately tied to its security and decentralized governance, bitcoin is the only asset to break the pressures of increasing demand on inflating supply. If gold doubles in price, gold miners can send double the miners down the shaft and inflate the supply twice as fast, thus decreasing demand and price. But no matter how many people are mining bitcoin, no matter how high the hash rate increases this month, the supply issuance remains at 6.25 bitcoin per block. Bitcoin is the only decentralized financial model in existence, and most likely the idea of a "decentralized stablecoin" is pure logical fallacy.

How can you distribute, secure and order transactions in a decentralized manner when the monetary policy itself is innately tied to the whims and dot plots of a seven-person centralized Federal

Reserve? Tether and the grander stablecoin system is a money market for the digital financial marketplace at large. By creating a robust, heavily margined ecosystem perpetuated and overwhelmingly supported specifically with inflows from dollar-denominated tokens, Tether and the like have pegged the short- and medium-term success of the bitcoin market to the dollar; when bitcoin retracts, arbitrage opportunities now exist for the dollar system to inflate further into the hard-capped, ever-demanded monetary system of Bitcoin. This pendulum-like market mechanism is the key component of the most important technological advancement in the finance world since the energy-based bimetallic and oil standards of yore. The world economy now finds itself irreversibly changed by the dawn of the bitcoin-dollar era.

Perhaps we should be less surprised by this realization than we are; the clues for an encouraged and implicit governmental policy approach to the dollarization of bitcoin are numerous. For starters, SHA-256, one of the secure hashing algorithms used in the Bitcoin network, was invented by the National Security Agency. But from strictly a financial and regulatory standpoint, the United States has significantly much more to lose than most with a net loss of purchasing power of the reserve dollar system.

Nearly four times as much profit was generated by Americans off bitcoin investments in 2020 (at around $4.1 billion) than the second closest nation (China at $1.1 billion). Would the US Securities and Exchange Commission (SEC) and Commodity Futures Trading Commission (CFTC) let American investors send a lofty percentage of our retail GDP value to an open-source network without a plan to conserve our purchasing economy? An ETF has yet to be approved by either of these regulating bodies, and yet they allow companies like MicroStrategy to take advantage of zero-interest rates and amass cheap debt to make, by all definitions and metrics, a speculative attack on the US dollar system. The six figures of bitcoin purchased on their balance sheet are now worth billions of dollars, surely raising the attention of their next-door neighbors in Langley Park. If the US was afraid of losing economic hegemonic status via bitcoin speculation, they would simply not allow exchanges and companies to do such dealings within their jurisdictions.

Regarding new financial regulations, legislation such as Basel III requires companies to have considerable holdings of on-sheet liquidity to offset speculations into commodities and assets could come. Any bank wanting to hold a bitcoin or gold position would also be required to hold an equal-part dollar to dollar-denominated value of their investments. This forces a net demand for dollars in the dollar system in spite of a loss of individual purchasing power due to inflation. There is certainly a future regulatory reckoning coming in the unregistered security sales of centralized protocols with known human leadership, but even Gary Gensler, the 33rd chair of the SEC, has determined Bitcoin and Nakamoto's innovation as "something real."

You can almost reductively view the consumption-based, ever-expanding debt bubble of fiat currency as a large balloon and the conservation-encouraging, hard-capped and distributed protocol of Bitcoin as a vacuum. By allowing somewhere for the United States monetary supply to inflate, we can pay off our immense debts without losing any demand or net-purchasing power via the congruent appreciation of bitcoin to the dollar. Pegging this new energy remittance market to the dollar during the increasingly important first decade of tokenized supply issuance has now forever linked the fates of the purchasing power of the dollar to the store of value properties of bitcoin. The United States has proven time and time again that it will do whatever is necessary to protect the purchasing power of the dollar system. The bitcoin-dollar is simply the next evolution of the energy-capital system needed for a functioning global economy. Perhaps the time has come for the Oracle of Omaha to take his own advice and never bet against America; the petrodollar died in March 2020, but like a phoenix rising from its oily ashes, so too was born the bitcoin-dollar.

𝑋

≼ Two ≽

The Stablecoin Monster

I know it pains some of your eyes even to see the word Ethereum printed, and while I respect that to a degree, the lessons learned by the extended cryptocurrency (unregistered securities) space are too important to ignore. Ignoring others, even as they potentially fall to centralizing forces, can only leave us ill-equipped to face the similar battle ahead. Only the naive should view this cooperation between the state and private financial entities as anything but a dire warning of what is about to come to Bitcoin.

Bitcoin is not immune to centralizing forces. Bitcoin is not immune to dollarization. There are many avenues in which Ethereum continues through this fork as a financial entity without any of the supposed benefits of being "the world's supercomputer." This same fate can come to fruition in Bitcoin, and while remaining a formidable financial asset, leave behind many of the taken-for-granted privacy qualities of physical notes. The state understands this to some degree, and the push for central bank digital currencies, or CBDCs, has only just been acknowledged in government offices across the globe. For some reason, this perfectly reasonable fear of loss of privacy and property rights innate to centralized money was only placed on money directly owned, and most importantly, issued by the state; the suddenly too-big-to-ignore stablecoin industry was left undisturbed, maturing to over $100 billion issued, mainly in the form of Ethereum ERC-20 tokens, and now finds itself seated at the Big Kid's Table as Ethereum prepares for their biggest consensus test yet – Proof-of-Stake.

Despite how Ethereum operates now, a proof-of-work model initially upheld consensus. From more or less the get-go, the foundation decided to encode a block height-triggered, exponential difficulty adjustment to ensure any changes the consortium wanted to make on the base layer could be done so without accounting for the incentives of the then-Ethereum miners. This action perverts the incentives away from block creation of the marketplace toward block validation from the system's stakeholders. The reason the Ethereum foundation was able to get away with this perversion every time is because they held the lion's share of the underlying asset, and thus their economic activity going to one side of the chain's fork meant everything. Whether or not you believe Ethereum to be started in good faith or not is beyond irrelevant now; the US dollar system just drank its milkshake.

The difficulty bomb was created for exactly this reason– the recent transfer from proof-of-work to Proof-of-Stake– but naivety left the keys to its detonator up for grabs. The weight of the coming fork between Eth2.0, PoWEth, ETC, etc., was suddenly in the hands of private corporations, cozying up to regulators and state departments by the hour. Which utopic variety of the supercomputer will Circle, the issuers of USDC, allow to exist? USDCEth? Already we see Antony Blinken, the Secretary of State, by protocol name calling out TornadoCash, an Eth-based privacy mixer, with coordination from Circle in blacklisting every address per request of the Treasury. This is a signpost and one that should be far from celebrated by freedom of speech maximalists.

But it is also a lesson in perverting incentives and presumptions about consensus-withholding corrupting forces. Ethereum could have been started 100% in good faith or 100% in bad faith, and the potential for a bottomless purse to capture market share while amassing such economic weight that it distorts consensus toward its preferred fork was always going to exist. But we are seeing something quite dire in the silencing of programmers' GitHub accounts who contributed code to the now-sanctioned TornadoCash. This is of course a far cry from a deposition, but should we be so carefree about who considers what to be protected speech? We might all understand a bitcoin transaction to be nothing but the expression of speech between two willing parties, but that doesn't mean our regulating bodies will. Interestingly enough, Blinken accused the party of directly working with the DPRK to launder funds; funds denominated not only in US dollars but using a privately-issued token. Decentralized stablecoins are a logical fallacy, arguably in how they eventually do rely on centralized consensus, but certainly in their ever-at-the-whim of the dozen Federal Reserve governors and extended board; all the benefits of the CBDC without any headache. In fact, a private-entity stablecoin probably reserves more rights for customer exclusion and asset seizure than a directly controlled government entity would.

You might claim Bitcoin suffers from a lack of features, but what it gains in simplicity is a far smaller target for centralizing forces to exploit. Could a bottomless coffer such as the Federal Reserve dollarize bitcoin or any of its layers in a similar fashion? Luckily, Bitcoin consensus is fork-adverse by nature, as opposed to fork-by-nature, the approach of the majority of today's smart contract platforms. Can an entity backed by the dollar pervert mining incentives enough to capture a large enough hash share to successfully censor transactions? Can an entity backed by the dollar create perverse incentives enough to dissuade proper custodial use of bitcoin? Can an entity backed by the dollar create malicious nodes in order to leak open-topographical network data to remove avenues for increased anonymity sets? Can an entity backed by the dollar scare developers enough into no longer publicly working on privacy tools? You bet they can.

The shared channel model of coming second layers such as Lightning will play a large role in bitcoin's ability to be a successful medium of exchange and generate the fees needed to sustain the network far beyond the block reward subsidiary. A shared-UTXO model allows liquidity providers and transactional, point-of-sale businesses a unique opportunity to take a large market share from legacy payment networks like Visa or Mastercard. Lightning at scale could offer near-instantaneous settlement with relatively private functionality. Sure, current institutional Lightning players like CashApp or Strike require Know-Your-Customer documents, utilize custodial dollars, and the pedestrian ubiquity of CCTV's and relative metadata eliminate much hope for truly private transactions in big box stores. But what happens when companies like Wal-Mart start to salivate over an alternative system in which they retain the 3% profits of the competing settlement networks, achievable simply by enticing their customers to use bitcoin for payments? Due to microscopic margins, even at the astronomical scale of a retailer like the Walton's, credit card companies often make more in a year simply processing payments for a business than the business itself makes. This parasitic behavior is perversely normalized and was left essentially unchanged for the last seventy years until the now-blossoming alternative to a generation of walled-garden settlement networks.

The problems with dollarizing Bitcoin's base layer, such as in the BIPs related to Taro or in the addition of stablecoins or other petrodollar-derivatives to Lightning itself, are both regulatory and systemic. Directly transferring US dollars between parties opens the possibility of making all bitcoin nodes be considered money transmitters. While not actually perverting consensus away from satoshi denominations toward dollars, dollar assets transferred along Bitcoin protocol rails and even hashed into its blockchain might require registration of all node runners, wallet providers, and software companies in the United States. The operational, systemic risks are neither obvious nor immediate but nevertheless important to consider. The US dollar is currently exhibiting volatility in both monetary supply and relative purchasing power, and the US government has reached barely manageable levels of debt. By dollarizing the on-and-off ramps, bitcoin trading pairs, custodial yields, exchange balances, and derivative collateral, users are forced to utilize dollar liquidity. No matter how fair of a supply distribution, those with short-term liquidity needs over time will transfer their stake to bigger players with only long-term liquidity needs. There is arguably no one in history with less short-term liquidity needs than the Federal Reserve. Stablecoin advocates within Bitcoin are fighting the dollar system with one arm while with the other spreading the greenback further and faster across the globe than ever.

While the current dilemmas of OFAC-compliance and centralizing block creation on Ethereum may read as a victory for the folks that understand security law, or those that view it as a bad faith project, what this really is is another victory for the US dollar over civil liberties, property rights, and freedom of speech. The current Eth2.0 staking contract was funded directly from a TornadoCash output. Are the billions of dollars locked into that contract now at risk of being seized, blacklisted or frozen by regulators and their stablecoin enforcers? For those that think these aren't Bitcoin problems and It Can't Happen Here, consider how sure the foundation must have felt in their kingdom; even a 70% pre-mined headstart wasn't enough to keep the greenbacks at bay. Bitcoin simply does not suffer from the same consensus failures as Ethereum; it suffers and strives uniquely on its own.

Being the leader of the pack is a comfort for sure, but as we look back at the oncoming US dollar system, we see yet another rider completely and utterly consumed by the gluttonous beast. We can see how they zigged when they might have zagged. We can see how the beast positioned itself – how it clawed and gained its ground. We spent so much time looking for CBDCs that we missed the private-entity stablecoin monster right in front of our eyes.

》《

≼ Three ≽

Castles Made of Sand Dollars

The story of Bitcoin has certainly had its fair share of nefarious characters, criminal activity, bad haircuts and worse wardrobes, and yet our antihero du jour has seemed to outdo them all. Sam Bankman-Fried, better known by his three-letter acronym, SBF, burst onto the scene at the peak of the 2017 bubble, founding Alameda Research just four years after graduating from an internship into a full-time position at Jane Street Capital. By the start of 2018, he had struck digital gold while taking advantage of the arbitrage opportunity presenting itself between the higher Asian-market bitcoin demand colloquially known as the "kimchi premium." By the end of the year, and after amassing a considerable fortune from this high-volume bitcoin/dollar spread, he officially moved to Hong

Kong, formally founding the derivatives exchange FTX the following spring, in May of 2019. The bitcoin network that SBF rode from rags to riches and back again was partially launched in direct response to the fiat money experiment rearing its ugly head in what is now known as the Great Financial Crisis of 2007-2009.

> "The Times 03/Jan/2009 Chancellor on brink of second bailout for banks."
> Satoshi Nakamoto, January 3, 2009

This now-infamous inscription in the genesis block made clear the inappropriate fractional reserve banking and subprime mortgage fiascos of our regulated banking industry were to be put to rest once and for all by this emergent monetary protocol; a completely transparent and decentralized ledger would de-incentivize fraud and prevent obfuscation of illicit activity. A new competitor to the dollar arose from the ashes of the meltdown, and with it, a new standard for financial fairness, complete with predictable issuance, controlled once and for all by the people, for the people. Yet in any system made with good intentions, sleazeballs like SBF and his bought and paid for political and media allies manage to find a way to hurt innocent people. Like most stories of intriguing fraudulent financial crimes, this one starts in the Bahamas, and ends with a tidal wave of asset liquidations and broken homes.

> "If you think the Bahamas has ruined your global tax system, you have a pretty terrible global tax system."
> Steven Dean, Summer 2020

The Bahamas seem innocuous enough, and yet there is a long history of US tax avoidance, complete with rum-running bootleggers during the prohibition era. The Caribbean banking centers, including the Bahamas and the Cayman Islands, as of August 2022, were the fourth largest foreign holders of Treasury securities, behind only Japan, China and the UK. Shortly after the time of its founding, FTX was fully taking advantage of the free money era begun with the 2008 crash and sustained by low-to-zero interest rates inaugurated by the Trump administration and further exacerbated by the lockdowns. An unprecedented pumping of all things dollar-denominated occurred, with real estate, stock indexes, bitcoin and a whole bunch of unregistered securities known as altcoins reaching new highs across the board. One month after the founding of FTX, Facebook's Mark Zuckerberg announced Libra, a digital currency based on a basket of international currencies; a novel take on stablecoins. This launched the stablecoin and CBDC race in earnest, and coincidentally enough, the Central Bank of the Bahamas became the first country to announce their own CBDC in October 2020. The Sand Dollar itself was pegged to the Bahamian dollar, which is itself pegged to the United States dollar, and thus with its government-sanctioned launch, the birth of the first central bank-issued stablecoin dollar came to be on the sandy beaches of SBF's new home.

> "What is the reserve currency of the crypto economy going to be? Right now it's unambiguously the USD. And interestingly it's USD whether or not you're looking at the American crypto economy."
> Sam Bankman-Fried, November 5, 2021

While the US government feigned fear of systemic risk at the time, the Chinese government understood the Libra project to be a backdoor dollarization of the G7 currencies proposed to be included in its basket, sped up by the high velocity available in digital payments and globalized by the borderless nature of the Facebook user base. The digital yuan was trialed in April 2021 with great haste in reaction to this development, and by the Winter Olympics 2022, had launched for foreign attendees in Beijing. Not to be outdone by these new-look, same-shit fiat cryptocurrencies, Bitcoin itself made financial history when President Nayib Bukele of El Salvador took to the stage at Bitcoin 2021 to announce the legal tender aspirations of his small but dollarized nation. On March 9, 2022, President Joe Biden signed Executive Order #14067 "Ensuring Responsible Development of Digital Assets," which included aspirations for mitigation of financial risks in digital asset markets, as well as a clause stating that within 210 days, the Attorney General, in consultation with the Secretary of the Treasury and the Chairman of the Federal Reserve, must provide a formal proposal for a government-issued CBDC.

By this point, the Bitcoin financial system had been utterly and properly dollar-ified, with billions of dollars in liquidity of dollar-denominated trading pairs making up the lion's share of market activity. The same can be said for the Ethereum network, which has seen its compliance-driven perversion by non-native assets taking the wheel from its token Ether, as stablecoin and other dollar derivatives now uphold the majority of economic weight of the system. Fortunately for Bitcoin, the consensus weight of the system is not manipulated by user stake, and thus the Bitcoin market has been seemingly unaffected – negatively anyway – by this decade-long development. At least until scammer Do Kwon and his Ponzi-scheme LUNA-UST disaster wreaked havoc on investors at the start of May of 2022.

> "[Crypto is] obviously serious... you want to do right by it in the regulatory space."
> President Bill Clinton, April 27, 2022

Only a few weeks after SBF hosted a keynote with politicians like former UK Prime Minister Tony Blair and President Bill Clinton at the FTX-organized Crypto Bahamas conference, the largest ever over-the-counter bitcoin purchase was announced by the LUNA team. Terraform Labs, the entity headed by Do Kwon, had begun a campaign to purchase bitcoin as a reserve asset in the event that their algorithmic stablecoin, UST, deviated from its $1 peg. Shortly before their collapse, the plan had ballooned to the lofty goal of stacking over $10 billion in the hardest digital commodity known to man. While it might feel like a decade ago, we all remember what happened next; the peg was attacked, the recently purchased bitcoin fortune was liquidated, CZ's Binance aptly halted all trading on LUNA and UST pairs – with notable exceptions to their own stablecoin BUSD – and Do Kwon seemingly fled to outside of US jurisdiction to Asia. Thus begins our first of many repeatable points of inquiry; where exactly did this bitcoin go? According to an audit released in November 2022, over 33,000 bitcoin were transferred to Binance and sold along with other assets while failing to defend the peg.

On May 13, SBF purchased a 7.6% stake in Robinhood, the trading platform that came under scrutiny for halting trading during the GameStop fiasco in early 2021. Bloomberg had reported that around 40% of Robinhood's revenue came directly from selling customer orders to firms such as Two Sigma and Citadel Securities. Citadel had been fined $700,000 in July 2020 for front-running trades placed by customers, and in September of that same year, Robinhood itself was questioned by the SEC for improperly informing clients of selling stock trades to known high-frequency trading firms. Previously in December 2020, Robinhood had agreed to pay $65 million to settle charges of repeated misstatements for failure to disclose their receipts of payments from said trading firms. When newly-elected Treasury Secretary Janet Yellen briefed President Joe Biden on this conflict of interest in February of 2021, she herself had to acquire an ethics waiver due to having received large speaking fees from Citadel LLC the year prior. SBF had disclosed this purchase via a filed Schedule 13-D form with the SEC, costing $648.3 billion dollars and giving him 2.8% voting power in their dual-class share structure under the entity Emergent Fidelity Technologies (a name said to be randomly generated).

"On July 13, Coinbase Exchange will be unifying USD and USDC order books. As part of the unification process, USDC order books will be merged under USD order books to create a better, more seamless trading experience with deeper liquidity for USD and USDC."

Coinbase Exchange Twitter, June 29, 2022

Circle, the entity behind the increasingly powerful USDC stablecoin, had previously expanded its international offerings with a subsidiary operation based in Bermuda with an announcement made on July 22, 2019. This entity, filed under the Digital Assets Business Act of 2018 ("DABA") meant that Circle was the first major stablecoin issuer to receive a Class F ("Full") DABA license that covered their operation of custody, payment services, exchange, trading and more financial services within the digital asset realm. Circle's other banking partners, Signet, Signature Bank and Silvergate Capital had made USD loans to Celsius, Voyager, Block Fi, Three Arrows Capital and Alameda Research. By the time this book was published, all had filed for bankruptcy. Two of their other business affiliates, Galaxy Digital and Genesis, have also reported massive losses in the FTX collapse, with rumors of further contagion effects coming. Coinbase, a publicly traded exchange under the ticker $COIN, announced in their Q2 2022 shareholder letter that nearly a third of total revenue was derived from interest on USD-denominated holdings, including a large USDC position. "Interest income was $33 million, up 211% compared to Q1. The increase was primarily driven by our USDC activity, as well as higher interest rates as we generate interest on fiat customer custodial funds...at the end of Q2, we had $6.2 billion in total $USD resources. In addition, we had $428 million of crypto assets." Previous to this announcement, as of May 3, 2022, interest on USDC holdings for twelve-month yields were up to 4.7%, while one-month yields were an even 4%. By November 16, 2022, USDC yields were down to 0% across all time frames.

> "Binance converts USDC --> BUSD, and we see the change in supplies. Thus begins the Second Great Stablecoin War."
>
> Sam Bankman-Fried, October 23, 2022

On September 4, 2022, Binance announced that they would be auto-converting all USDC, USDP, and TUSD, three major dollar stablecoins, into their self-issued BUSD, effective in just twenty-five days. This led to major concerns about Binance's solvency, and in the following months saw the largest known outflows of bitcoin in the exchange's history, eclipsing even March 2020's black swan bottom. On October 11, 216 days after Biden's EO with the aforementioned 210-day clause, BNY Mellon, the world's largest custodian bank with over $43 trillion on the books, and coincidentally the custodian of Circle's reserves backing USDC, announced the launch of their digital asset custody program. With over 20% of the world's investable assets, the bank founded by the first Secretary of the Treasury Alexander Hamilton was also formerly listed as a partner in the FedNow pilot. Despite these institutional developments, a continued bear market weighed heavily on the now-plummeting bitcoin price. Paradoxically, more and more Bitcoin hashrate poured onto the network. These concurrent movements saw Bitcoin's hash price plummet to an all-time low, spurring a massive liquidation of bitcoin liabilities off mining operators' books. On October 26, Core Scientific, then the largest Bitcoin mining operation in the world, filed for bankruptcy with millions of dollars in debt liabilities, thousands of ASICs, and yet in their filings, held only 24 bitcoin when the circus came to town. Where exactly did all this bitcoin go? On that same day, barely two weeks before the FTX collapse, Binance saw its largest single-day outflow, with 71,579 coins, totaling over $1.1 billion in dollar terms. This pushed net outflows to nearly 95,000 coins from the world's largest exchange since just that July. Again, where exactly did all this bitcoin end up? The very next day, October 27, 2022, SBF appeared on The Big Whale and announced future plans for FTX to launch their very own stablecoin.

> "CIA and Mossad and pedo elite are running some kind of sex trafficking entrapment blackmail ring out of Puerto Rico and Caribbean islands. They are going to frame me with a laptop planted by my ex gf who was a spy. They will torture me to death."
> Nikolai Mushegian, October 28, 2022

On October 24, 2022, the MakerDAO approved a community proposal to custody nearly $1.6 billion USDC with Coinbase Prime. Four days later, Nikolai Mushegian, the co-founder of MakerDAO and inventor of Rai, a DAI-fork stablecoin, tweeted his life was in danger due to a Caribbean island blackmail ring supposedly backed by Israeli and US intelligence agents. Three days later, on Halloween, the 29-year-old coder Mushegian was found dead, having drowned in the sea off Condado Beach in Puerto Rico. Two days later, on November 2, 2022, reporter Ian Allison released findings that over a third of all assets – around $5.8 billion of $14.6 billion – on the balance sheet of SBF's Alameda

Research were intrinsically (and soon to be fatally) linked to FTX's exchange token FTT. A "bank" run commenced, and after three days of nearly $6 billion in withdrawals, FTX was left with literally one single bitcoin. Where exactly did all this bitcoin go? The next day in an interview with *Fortune*, Coinbase founder and CEO Brian Armstrong made note that USDC will become the de facto central bank digital currency in the US.

> "The policymakers in the US will set the framework that need to be followed so that the private market will actually create the solutions, and USD coin has been on a really rapid rise ... the regulatory environment is one of the biggest unlocks we're going to have in terms of growing this industry and perhaps even getting the prices to go back up in the right direction"
>
> Brian Armstrong, November 3, 2022

On November 6, CZ announced it would liquidate the remaining portion of FTT it had acquired from exiting FTX's equity, having received around $2.1 billion in BUSD and FTT. Minutes after his announcement, Caroline Ellison, SBF's partner and CEO of Alameda Research, offered to purchase the tokens at $22 each in an over-the-counter fashion. By November 8, CZ and SBF had a phone call and seemingly came to a tentative deal for acquisition, reserving the right to back out of the deal at any time, while interestingly also leaving both US-based proprietary exchanges, Binance.us and FTX.us, outside the scope of the deal. That evening, FTX officially suspended all asset withdrawals. As part of the conditions of the acquisition, SBF was forced to open the FTX books and show the bottom of his pockets; seeing more sand than dollars, CZ backed out of the deal.

> "Liquidating our FTT is just post-exit risk management, learning from LUNA. We gave support before, but we won't pretend to make love after divorce. We are not against anyone. But we won't support people who lobby against other industry players behind their backs. Onwards."
>
> CZ, November 6, 2022

On November 7, 2022, the SEC officially deemed LBRY, or Library Coin, an unregistered security offering, setting a devastating precedent throughout the extended cryptocurrency market.

In the United States District Court for the District of New Hampshire, the memorandum and order read, "The Securities and Exchange Commission (SEC) contends that LBRY, Inc. offered and sold unregistered securities in violation of Section 5 of the Securities Act of 1933," the act colloquially known as the Howey Test. Due to LBRY reserving a pre-mine of nearly 400 million LBC tokens, and the knowledge of the company to date having spent approximately half of its pre-mined LBC, the SEC determined common enterprise complete with a lack of disclosure and proper filing of their now alleged security offering through required channels in the Gary Gensler-chaired SEC. The implications of this filing sent shockwaves throughout the pre-mined token industry and set a worrisome precedent for those exchanges listing these tokens as well as the entities behind their issuance. Conveniently, the next day was November 8, the midterm elections in the US, with the balance of the Senate and the House (and perhaps the regulatory path of the digital asset industry) once again at stake. Searching for FTX on FEC.gov brings up 456 individual campaign contributions from SBF, CEO Ryan Salame, and others. Salame's contributions total over $14 million toward GOP candidates, while SBF's "effective altruism" contributed over $20 million in donations to DNC politicians. Having been the second leading donor to the Biden campaign, by the time the final tallies from election night rolled in, SBF's bankroll had finally caught up with his morals, and he found himself nearly completely bankrupt. By November 9, the day after the elections, SBF had reportedly lost 94% of his net worth, down to $1 billion from more than $15 billion, leaving him (according to the Bloomberg Billionaire Index) with the largest single-day loss by a person. Early in the morning of November 10, SBF took to Twitter to explain what happened, writing, "I'm sorry. That's the biggest thing. I fucked up, and should have done better," before making a specific note that "THIS IS ALL ABOUT FTX INTERNATIONAL, THE NON-US EXCHANGE. FTX US USERS ARE FINE!"

> "The administration ... has consistently maintained that without proper oversight, cryptocurrencies risk harming everyday Americans. ... The most recent news further underscores these concerns and highlights why prudent regulation of cryptocurrencies is indeed needed."
>
> White House Press Secretary Karine Jean-Pierre, November 10, 2022

On the eleventh day of the eleventh month, FTX and Alameda Research officially filed for Chapter 11 bankruptcy protection, and SBF stepped down as CEO. In addition, 130 affiliated companies connected or associated with FTX also commenced voluntary proceedings under Chapter 11. The tide had gone out, and nearly everyone involved got caught swimming naked, as a near-endless tidal wave of dollar-denominated liquidations made quick work of SBF's Caribbean empire. While the first trickles of a dollar CBDC may have started in the Bahamas, the monsoon of coming regulation and contagion of the Second Great Stablecoin War is far from over. The dollar, having fallen 10% off 35-year DXY highs since September, looks for new ways to innovate and further dollarize markets across the globe. On

November 15, just four days after the SBF tsunami crashed to shore, BNY Mellon, as well as a dozen or so other banking institutions, announced the start of a twelve-week digital dollar pilot program with the Federal Reserve Bank of New York. On the very same day, Block Fi announced plans for bankruptcy filings, only five months after taking a $250 million loan from FTX, and Circle announced users would now be able to settle payments by accepting Apple Pay.

Later that month, on November 30, SBF was set to appear in a New York Times event, sponsored by Accenture, alongside Secretary Yellen, Meta CEO Mark Zuckerberg, Ukraine President Volodymyr Zelensky, BlackRock CEO Larry Fink, TikTok CEO Shou Chew, former Vice President Michael Pence, Amazon CEO Andy Jassy, Netflix Co-founder and CEO Reed Hastings, New York City Mayor Eric Adams, and others. Tickets for the event were listed at $2,499 per attendee. While appearing to be riding the wave of the booming digital asset revolution, gathering celebrity endorsements and political allies alike, it turns out SBF was drowning in debt and capital misallocation amongst the loud, mainstream praise. Bitcoin tends to be a ballast of truth, bringing all sorts of ballooning fraud rushing to the surface. FTX and Alameda Research will take their place amongst the seemingly too-big-to-sink players that ended up doing just that. They will certainly not be the last. However the following weeks, months, and years play out, it is clear that SBF was but a small fish in an ocean-sized, dollarized pond. And as he quickly found out, there is always a bigger fish.

> "At some point I might have more to say about a particular sparring partner, so to speak. But you know, glass houses. So for now, all I'll say is: well played; you won."
> Sam Bankman-Fried, November 10, 2022

𝄞

Four

The Nakamoto Accord

The greatest heist in the history of money did not occur in the branch of a bank, nor behind the vaults of a precious metal custodian, but rather in an otherwise innocuous hotel lobby in New York City in the Fall of 1985.

Fourteen years prior, Richard Milhouse Nixon shocked the world by publicly announcing the severing of the gold-dollar peg; a ceremonious move that all but confirmed what the market had already learned many times over in the decades previous. Public trust in the peg had eroded, with sound reason, infamously in President Eisenhower's Executive Order 6102 in 1933, ordering the seizure of citizens' gold, causing Charles de Gaulle to send the French Navy in February of 1965 sailing across the Atlantic to convert their US dollar holdings back into gold, and further publicly in the collapse of the London Gold Pool. Theoretically, the expansion and growth of the Bretton Woods system was limited by the supply issuance of its pegged value, in this case, the extraction rate of mined gold. In 1964, short-term interest rates were below 4%, having shrunk from wartime debt and post-WWII bubbles in credit expansion. By January 1970, short-term interest rates had more than doubled to 8.9%, mainly an effect of the US dollar oligarchs attempting to preserve foreign and domestic wealth within the Bretton Woods system. By rapidly raising the interest paid on short-term bonds or treasury bills, the Federal Reserve of the US was handsomely paying investors beyond the means of the growth of the gold-peg itself to ensure faith in said peg. In hindsight of course this makes little-to-no mathematical or economic sense – a running theme in the rate manipulation of the world's reserve currency, and thus the world's economy.

By 1969, Nixon had inherited a recession from his predecessor Lyndon B. Johnson, primarily due to the Vietnam War, the uncertainty after John F. Kennedy's assassination, and his "Great Society" spending. By the end of the fiscal year of 1970, GDP had shrunk to $1.07 trillion, GDP per capita to $5,234, netting the first negative print in a decade, coming in at -0.28% from the year previous. In order to stimulate growth, pay for the now floundering Vietnam War, and (as always) to make a select Cantilionare class rich, the US began rapidly expanding the monetary supply; in one decade, from 1965 to 1975, the M1 doubled. From 1970 through 1992, the Federal Reserve did not let a single year pass without changing the Fed rate, and in fact averaged nearly five changes a year. Oddly enough, there were no rate changes in 1993, holding strong at 3%, before restarting their manipulation game, averaging nearly four changes per year from 1994 through 2008. At first, this gold-peg severing and rate hike seemed to work, with the US averaging over 4% annual GDP growth from 1971 through the start of 1974. Eventually, rates lowered, and due to inflation no longer being limited to gold deposits, this credit expansion mutated into inflationary effects, with monetary expansion far outpacing demand for the now-debased dollar; a high level of inflation remained throughout the 1970s and into the early 1980s.

The anti-hero of our story, the man responsible for the most rapid and intense rate manipulation seen until 2022, Paul Volcker, would be nominated by Nixon's successor, Democrat Jimmy Carter, in 1979. In a trend that would continue throughout the ensuing decades, he was later renominated by a successor from the other side of the aisle, Hollywood actor Ronald Reagan. Volcker was tasked with eliminating the inflationary effects of monetary expansion of the 1970s, and that he did. Reagan, a figurehead for trickle-down economics, signed a budget that had the US government spending more than their tax receipts, increasing demand for the dollar and bringing 3% GDP growth between 1983 and 1984, with an account deficit barely above 3% of GDP. Volcker did something seemingly unbelievable at the time, and certainly impossible before the global fiat experiment began in earnest with the Nixon Shock, and raised the short-term rate above 10%. The US dollar soared relative to the other G5 nations at the time, with the Eurozone seeing a -0.7% GDP contraction, complete with a lofty trade surplus. Japan and West Germany were buying up US bonds, Treasury notes, Treasury bills, and just about anything they could get their hands on with these large surpluses from a strong dollar and double-digit rates, and in turn financing our debt at their growth's expense. Eventually, this would hurt US growth domestically due to the innate high cost of domestic products being made on dollar-denominated accounts, and soon forcing foreign exchange trade wars.

The DXY, or the comparative-strength index of the US dollar, broke 160 on February 1, 1985, against a basket of currencies representing the most important central banks of the world. From 1980 through 1985, the US dollar appreciated over 50% against the Japanese Yen, the Deutsche Mark, the French Franc, and the British Pound – the four biggest economies at the time in a post-WWII world. While GDP growth was negative in 1980, coming in -0.26% annually at $2.85 trillion, by 1984, the US GDP had expanded rapidly to over $4 trillion, hitting an expansion of 7.24% by the end of the fiscal year alone. In March of 1985, previous to any meeting between the G5 nations, the USD/GBP reached a high unmatched for over three decades, and by September, one US dollar exchanged for over 242 Japanese Yen. Volcker, representing the United States, called for coordinated central bank intervention, and invited his equivalents at the central banks of West Germany, the United Kingdom, France, and Japan to gather in the lobby of The Plaza Hotel in New York City. **On September 22, 1985, the Plaza Accord began, when all the king's**

horses and all the king's men tried to put the world economy back together again.

Agreeing to lower the exchange rate of the dollar 10-12% in as little as six weeks, the US dollar cratered over 50% relative to the remaining G5 members, falling from 242 JPY/USD at the time of the meeting to 153 JPY/USD by 1986 and finally to 120 JPY/USD in 1988. So why exactly did Paul Volcker and the US government agree to this? Why would a country willingly devalue its currency on the world stage? The effects of relative dollar depreciation obviously benefit developing countries greatly, with global cooperation and newly-possible globalized trade directly leading to new economic forces and new purchasing economies such as Brazil. By why would the dollar being depreciated be a net-benefit for the US? For starters, too strong of a dollar means US domestic industries are less competitive with foreign industries, leading to a fear of poor employment and thus decreasing GDP growth and potential for credit expansion. By increasing capital mobility and gaining inroads into emerging manufacturing machines such as Japan, the US was able to expand growth and increase both the user base and monetary velocity of the US dollar significantly. The actual agreements were unique to each country involved; West Germany cut taxes and agreed to increase labor force; the UK agreed to cut public expenditure, increase the labor force, and increase the weight of the private sector to the public sector; Japan agreed to open markets globally, set a true Yen exchange, increase the labor force, and deregulate and liberalize their formidable internal public markets. The US simply agreed to debase their currency, with the desired effects of labor market growth and fairer competition within the now-booming global manufacturing economy.

> "What gave the Plaza Accord its historic importance was a multitude of firsts. It was the first time central bankers agreed to intervene in the currency markets, the first time the world set target rates, the first time for the globalization of economies, and the first time each nation agreed to adjust its own economies. Sovereignty was exchanged for globalization."
>
> Brian Twomey

The United States post-Plaza Accord meant a weaker dollar, a weaker dollar meant US exports became more affordable due to the favorable exchange rate, and a favorable exchange rate meant the once cheap imports from European nations and Japan were suddenly more expensive. Japan continued down the path of lowering rates, immense credit expansion, and eventually took the belt of the world's leading creditor nation. This cheap, depreciating Yen led to a massive decrease in consumption of domestic goods, thus leading to a massive asset bubble and furthering a housing bubble; these bubbles eventually popping escorted Japan into what is known now as The Lost Decade. Succeeding Volcker, along came the appropriately named Alan Greenspan, the thirteenth and longest-tenured chairman of the Federal Reserve. Greenspan was initially nominated by Reagan, a Republican, and then renominated in a back-and-forth bipartisan fashion by George H. W. Bush, Bill Clinton, and later George W. Bush. In 1989, rates remained above 10%, but GDP growth shrank by the end of 1991 by ten basis points to $6.15 trillion, and by September of 1992 the short-term rate had collapsed to nearly 3% and the DXY shrunk to a then-new low of 78.8, which would remain the low until the start of the Great Financial Crisis in September of 2007. Greenspan was forced to raise short-term rates, doubling from 3% in 1992 to 6.73% in 2000, and the effects were immediately apparent; from 1992 through the start of the new millennium, annual GDP never went below 2.5%, and at the end of 2000, GDP broke $10 trillion, with GDP per capita at $36,330.

The 1990s were a unique period in the history of the United States' economy. Unlike previous growth found in the 1960s, 1970s, and 1980s, the debt to GDP ratio crossed 50% in June of 1989; the first time in a post-World War world since June of 1962. It peaked at 65.3% in March of 1995, and was marginally lowered to a still-staggering 54% by March of 2001. The main engine of 1990s growth was a mass improvement in both production and productivity of information technology manufacturing and domestic investment in said IT equipment. Between 1990 and 1995, real GDP grew at an average annual rate just below 2.5%, significantly down from the over 4% growth between 1983 and 1989. Robert Solow, a notable economist of the age, famously said, "You can see the computer age everywhere but in the productivity statistics." Multifactor productivity gains barely grew at all, averaging five basis points per year. Between 1996 and 2000, GDP growth again began to pick up, with short-term rates lowering from 6.29% in December of 1994 to below 4.9% in May of 1999. Multifactor productivity grew 1.3% annualized from the midpoint of the decade through 2000, with labor productivity growing over 2.5% in services and 2.3% in the manufacturing sector. The Plaza Accord's effects of the opening of Japan's industrial market, as well as the now-emerging formidable China lead to a decreased price of semiconductors, as well as new levels of processing efficiencies.

> "Over the past decade, economists have reached a consensus that (i) the trend rate of growth of labor productivity in the US economy increased in the mid-1990s and (ii) the underlying cause of that increase was technological innovations in semiconductor manufacturing that increased the rate of decrease of semiconductor prices. This productivity acceleration is remarkable because, unlike most of its predecessors, it continued with only a minor slowdown during the most-recent recession."
> The 1990s Acceleration in Labor Productivity: Causes and Measurement by Richard G. Anderson and Kevin L. Kliesen

In November of 2000, the Fed rate sat at 6.6%, and yet one year later, immediately after the

September 11 events of 2001, the short-term rate fell to just 2%, with a low of 1% in June of 2003. Despite lowering rates, the DXY rose relatively to a peak of 120 in January of 2002, before descending for the rest of the decade to a low of 71 in June of 2008. By the end of 2007, the US GDP broke $14.4 trillion, with a GDP per capita just below $50,000.

When looking simply at these metrics, one could incorrectly postulate that the US economy was thriving.

Enter Ben Bernanke, the 14th chair of the Federal Reserve, serving from 2006 to 2014, and again, nominated by a Republican, Bush Jr., and renominated by a Democrat, Obama. In 2001, the US debt stood at just $5.8 Trillion at 55% debt to GDP ratio, and yet by 2009 had doubled to $11.9 trillion, with a staggering 82% debt to GDP ratio. A lot happened between the events of 2001 and the invasion of the Middle East and the market action now known as the Great Financial Crisis, spread out between late 2007 into early 2009. Much has been written on Bear Stearns, Lehman Brothers, and the collapse of the subprime retail market, but less on the downstream effects of the banker bailouts and the rapid rate reduction led by the future-Nobel economist Bernanke. In February of 2008, the

Economic Stimulus Act passed, accompanied by an innocuous price tag of $152 billion. Between October 2008 and November 2008, the short-term rate fell nearly 50%, from 4.32% to 2.36%. By December 2008, the rate sat at 1.77%, only to fall another near 50% in a month, to just above 1% by January 2009. One month later, in February 2009, only one year after the last bailout, the American Recovery and Reinvestment Act passed the now-Democrat led Senate, but this time with a staggering price tag of $831 billion. 2008 saw nominal growth at 0.12%, but by the end of 2009, the US GDP shrank to $14.4 trillion, down nearly -2.6% from the year prior. Rates remained effectively at 0% for the remainder of Bernanke's term, and through the Janet Yellen appointment by Obama in 2014 as the 15th chair of the Federal Reserve. She remained in office until 2018, and was not renominated by Donald Trump, only later to become the 78th Treasury Secretary under Joe Biden. Despite low rates, and after hitting a local low of 72 in April 2011, the DXY rose to 100 by November 2015; more importantly, the debt to GDP ratio crossed 100% in 2013, at nearly $17 trillion. By 2016, before Republicans took back the executive branch, the debt to GDP ratio crossed 105%, sitting at an incomprehensible $20 trillion.

Jerome Powell, the 16th chair of the Federal Reserve, was nominated by the Republican Trump after Yellen's tenure ended, only to be renominated by Democrat Biden in late 2021. In March of 2020, elected officials and non-elected officials alike unilaterally decided to impose catastrophic lockdowns on the United States economy due to pandemic threats, and shortly after the announcement, stock indexes, gold, oil and bitcoin all crashed in synchronicity. Immediate action was deemed necessary, and the CARES Act was passed unanimously that same month; this stimulus came with an outrageous $2.2 trillion price tag. By the end of 2020, GDP had shrunk to $20.9 trillion, down nearly -3.40% from the year prior. With the economy still locked down and considered in need of further stimulus, the Consolidated Appropriations Act of 2021 was passed for an additional $900 billion in December of 2021. Three months later, another $1.9 trillion was earmarked as the American Rescue Plan passed. Across the world, other central banks followed suit, with a mass reduction of inflation rates, including some actually going negative. Despite their best efforts to gaslight it out of existence, the highly inflationary effects of these stimulus packages led to a weakening dollar in the form of rising CPI and expressed in bubbling dollar-denominated asset prices. By May of 2021, the DXY had fallen to 89.

Realizing the effectiveness of Volcker's rate hikes of the mid-1980s, Powell began to raise rates, starting with sub-100 basis point moves. This action, plus an increase in government spending, and global short-term rates at, near, or below zero, the US dollar began to surge. In the fastest month-over-month hikes in US history, Powell brought rates above 4.25%, causing the DXY to surge to nearly 115 by the fall of 2022; the dollar index hit thirty-year highs not seen since Volcker. The Japanese Yen has again fallen, the British Pound nearly lost dollar parity, the Euro sunk below 97 cents, and a handful of near and even actual hyperinflationary events occurred across the globe. **Again, the United States finds itself with all the leverage over the world economy, except this time, it is over-leveraged against itself.** Unlike 1985, the US finds itself $33 trillion in debt, with a disastrous 124% Debt to GDP ratio. The mechanics of an increasing Fed rate means an increase in the debt service needed to be paid. Raising rates a la Volcker to double digits would effectively mean a default, as the service owed each year on our debt would far outpace our GDP growth. Rates will eventually need to be lowered, or money will need to be printed; there is no other option. You cannot taper a Ponzi.

Debt is not the only notable difference to 1985: there is China and a new financial instrument and asset class. Bitcoin is best known for its capped supply and eventual peak of 21 million coins issued, but perhaps the more useful quality in today's economy is its stable yet disinflationary monetary policy. When looking at Bitcoin under the guise of John Nash's *Ideal Money*, the concept of an ideal issuance rate, N, is surely bested by an algorithmic, step-function decrease, or $N/2$, colloquially known as a halving. The US cannot afford to raise rates to double figures, and thus must rely on another enticing issuance rate to retain capital in the dollar system and avoid unwanted effects from the massive money printing of the 2020s. Much like 1985, the US finds itself with extreme financial power over the Eurozone, now the ECB, over Japan, our second-biggest creditor, and the rest of the world banks' that rely on dollar-denominated purchasing power. The failed Libra project, a basket of currencies proposed by Facebook, a private-entity arm posing significant national security concerns for the US government, was an attempt at backward-dollarizing these G7 nations. By setting an exchange rate and creating a token based on the relative strength of said central bank currencies, Libra was essentially a failed Plaza Accord 2.0. The Central Bank of China realized this immediately, and despite US government officials admirably and publicly feigning fear of the Libra undermining the dollar's strength, speed-tracked their own digital yuan, successfully launching the first CBDC in 2021.

The future rates of note will be simple in a bitcoin-dollar economy; US stablecoin yield, US short-term interest rate, and Bitcoin's supply issuance. The Nakamoto Accord would be the understanding that it would be in the best interest of Japan, the UK, the EU, and the United States, to agree upon a debasement of United States currency in the form of debt jubilee, freeing Japanese creditors from an inflating dollar, purchasing debts from an imploding UK bond market, supplying the ECB with capital to pay off food and energy debts, and allowing the US to remain the economic hegemony of the world over China and Russia. The US is going to need to print money or lower rates eventually, but the EU, the UK, and Japan need to do it now. By pegging the dollar to Bitcoin's limitless demand potential and by setting algorithmic interests for stablecoin wallets, the US can further capital mobility, increase the dollar system network effects, and further diminish the inflationary action of a run-away monetary supply. **The US dollar and Bitcoin continue to evolve together, making unlikely bedfellows for those that refuse to learn from history.**

At the end of the day, economically speaking, Bitcoin is a settlement network, and one that will one day price out the vast majority of users from being able to afford base layer transactions. Yet access to Bitcoin's stable monetary rate, in the form of bitcoin-backed dollar instruments, or even second-layer solutions, can still be profoundly beneficial if looked at as a neutral central bank. Bitcoin's inability to be manipulated by central bankers may develop into its most important feature by far, and one with profound implications on the success of whoever can tether themselves to it first. When asked who should succeed Powell as the next Federal Reserve chair in 2021, Peter Thiel infamously, and perhaps prophetically, stated "Satoshi Nakamoto." Lucky for us, there are no consensus mechanisms to nominate anyone to manipulate the supply issuance of Bitcoin, and once the 33rd epoch begins, a new era of financial stability will be born.

𝕏

⋘ Five ⋙

Ideal Banking

"The special commodity or medium that we call
money has a long and interesting history. And
since we are so dependent on our use of it and
so much controlled and motivated by the wish
to have more of it or not to lose what we have
we may become irrational in thinking about it
and fail to be able to reason about it like about
a technology, such as radio, to be used more or
less efficiently."

John Forbes Nash, Jr.

Money is a technological tool that humans developed organically out of the necessity of bargaining axioms such as time and space. Many of the financial services that exist today have risen to meet the need of an evolving market, and yet at its most reductive, the modern banking system still represents supply and demand via sellers and buyers. This remains true even when looking into the complicated circuit of the US banking system, including the regional banks providing mortgages for first-time buyers, to corporate debt obligations from large private American banks to the issuance of government bonds by the Treasury. Only by examining the monetary flow in a logical manner within our current system can we begin to present coherent alternatives to the status quo of a select few holding the special privilege as a world reserve currency debt pardoner. At the center of the circuit of the US banking system sits the Federal Reserve and the Treasury – a proprietary black box chip that controls both the current (short-term and overnight interest rates) and voltage (the issuances of US Treasuries, "USTs").

> "The root problem with conventional currency is all the trust that's required to make it work. The central bank must be trusted not to debase the currency, but the history of fiat currencies is full of breaches of that trust. Banks must be trusted to hold our money and transfer it electronically, but they lend it out in waves of credit bubbles with barely a fraction in reserve. We have to trust them with our privacy, trust them not to let identity thieves drain our accounts."
>
> Satoshi Nakamoto

The reserve asset at the bottom of the stack of the US economy is not the US dollar but rather US Treasuries. Offshore dollar markets such as the eurodollar have long operated under the illusion of dollar creation by these European banks without hardly touching US-issued government debt. The Treasury issues debt in the form of USTs to be sold to private banks, which later create credit via dollars in their customer accounts in order to finance the budget of the US government, as well as service any outstanding national debt. The idea of issuing new debt to service old debt would seem illogical, and in many ways it is, yet becomes far more conceivable with the proper understanding that not all debt is created equal. Debt, at least in the Treasury issuance example above, is demarcated by both the percentage of profit generated as yield and the duration until said bond reaches maturity. Historically, and perhaps logically, the longer the duration (twenty years vs. one year), the higher the yield (2.4% vs 1.2%, using real rates from March 2022). The most liquid denomination of government debt is short-term Treasury bills, referred to as T-bills, which are any bonds with a maturity date of less than one year; generally, the yields on those bonds are most directly influenced by short-term federal funding rates. When the government wants to sell more debt, it can increase the yield on these T-bills by increasing the short-term interest rate on offer, driving yield-seeking capital back into the US banking system in search of profit. When rates rise, the cost to borrow increases and these new debt instruments soak up excess dollar liquidity.

Conversely, when rates fall, the cost to borrow decreases, and thus the demand for personal debt increases. To put it simply, if rates are at or near zero, more people will take on debt due to the negligible additional economic cost of eventually paying it back. When rates are higher, and there is market-high yield to be made on simply loaning dollars to the government by purchasing government-issued securities, there is little available supply to be loaned out and even less demand due to the high costs of borrowing. The issue with this credit-debt boom-bust cycle is that it is levered by trusted third parties, culminating with a buyer and lender of last resort at the modern Federal Reserve – who are in fact actually limited in their ability to manipulate the short end of the yield curve. The yield curve demonstrates the different yields offered by the bond market, denoted by their duration. When there is unexpected and excessive relative volatility within short-term interest rates, the yield curve can invert, meaning short-term debt now pays a higher yield than long-term bonds. If simply held to maturity, sometimes as long as 30 years, Treasury bonds will never yield a material loss, but if short-term liquidity needs strike a bank in the form of depositors withdrawing, banks are forced to sell and realize a loss.

The health and efficiency of the US banking system can be measured in how volatile short-term interest rates are, the state of the yield curve, foreign and domestic interest in government-issued bonds, and the discrepancy between outstanding liabilities and reserves – be it securities or cash.

> "It's not all about payments. We will have exchanges forever. We will have banks forever."
>
> Calle

Did you notice that at no point above were payments even mentioned? Bitcoin in its current state is not necessarily ready to replace the dollar as a global medium of exchange, which takes advantage of financial services to scale over time and space, but it is potentially poised to replace USTs as a world reserve asset and an inter-banking settlement network. For Bitcoin to service the many functions of a banking system, there needs to be further tooling beyond the peer-to-peer payment networks innate to the base layer and the Lightning Network, the most discussed second layer. Paper money represents dollars as cash, a physical bearer asset for settling debt obligations, yet the majority of US dollars today exist solely as credit in a user's account balance at a trusted third party such as a bank. In stark contrast, Bitcoin itself contains zero account balances and instead relies on a UTXO model: Non-fungible unspent transaction outputs that when signed and spent can transfer fungible satoshis, the atomic unit of bitcoin, between wallet addresses. The address balance of your wallet is an aggregation of the multiple UTXOs associated with your private key. By sharing a UTXO between two or more parties, typically in the form of Lightning channels, Layer 2 payment solutions create near-instant, probabilistically trustless settlements allowing for account balances. By taking a UTXO and creating a shared channel with a peer, you create the functions of credit and debt within the Bitcoin network. Some instances of LN even allow sub-satoshi denominations such as "msats" – a literally unrecognizable unit on the base layer, and thus only existing as a form of credit or debt. Due to the nature of Layer 2 solutions having the ability to simulate credit and debt, these services enable a trustless iteration of yield via routing fees and trust-minimized financial services akin to the traditional banking system. Tooling built on top of Bitcoin can create analogs to legacy loan, yield, and liquidity-sharing services. Unfortunately, a significant aspect of the trustlessness of Layer 2s being able to finalize and settle back to the mainchain is an open topological network and an ever-surveilled open ledger, significantly reducing the capacity for private financial exchanges.

> "Actually there is a very good reason for Bitcoin-backed banks to exist, issuing their own digital cash currency, redeemable for Bitcoins. Bitcoin itself cannot scale to have every single financial transaction in the world be broadcast to everyone and included in the block chain.
> There needs to be a secondary level of payment systems which is lighter weight and more efficient."
>
> Hal Finney

Chaumian mints were invented by cryptographer and mathematician David Chaum in a 1982 paper titled "Blind Signatures For Untraceable Payments." Chaumian mints utilize blind signatures to represent ecash in mint-specific denominations to create near-perfect privacy within the federation. This newly-found privacy is at the expense of reserve asset custody and potential economic debasement depending on both the coding of the mint instance as well as malicious actions from mint authority signatures. This is a situation nearly identical to the downsides of using a legacy financial institution. Ecash uses a similar token mechanic to bitcoin in that while a single wallet can appear to contain an aggregate account balance, in reality the ecash wallet balance is actually distributed among many iterations of common denominations of ecash tokens issued by the mint. The mint itself is completely unaware of the account which funded the initial issuance of ecash, and at redemption merely sees that it had previously validated this token via a blind signature. When using any privacy-preserving payment protocol, there are always two anonymity sets: inside and outside the protocol. While a Chaumian mint can offer near-perfect privacy when transacting within the federated mint itself, an external settlement from the mint can be noticed with a low number of user withdrawals, unassuming metadata collection, and a multitude of poor operational security choices by users. A user could generate ecash from a Chaumian mint instance via a relatively private sender-side LN payment, take the newly generated tokens and fund another outbound sender-side LN payment with zero ability for the mint to generate user account balance information, nor associated metadata with proper external privacy technique. With cheap, near-instant, and perfectly private payments, if authored correctly, Chaumian mints can bridge the gaps between Layer 2 balances and even base layer UTXOs.

Chaumian mint construction types differ mainly in two ways: the federation construction itself and the ecash token denominations it issues. A federation can contain a single signature with administrative access to issuing its ecash, as well as having the ability to sign for the mint's reserve asset when processing withdrawals. A federation can also enable multi-signature capabilities to similar mint duties, distributing responsibilities away from a single point of failure to a quorum of trusted third parties. Ecash token denominations are unique to the mint, but theoretically decided at launch of the instance. In lossy parallel to Bitcoin's UTXO model, there are no account balances but rather aggregates of ecash tokens issued as common denominations (think $5, $10, and $20 notes). These common denominations allow for greater fungibility and far greater anonymity sets within the mint, especially when combined with issuance validation via blind signatures. All of these decisions, including the relative issuance per reserve asset – say ecash token per satoshi – are to be made by the founders of the Chaumian mint, generally upon its genesis. Cashu is a popular, open-source, single-signature instance (created by open-source developer Calle) that is capable of being spun up quickly, leaning on tooling such as LNBits to create fast and easy operability with users already on the Lightning Network. Fedimint, a multi-signature instance, allows for a more decentralized mint consensus among federation members, creating more administrative checks within the mint when issuing ecash tokens and when eventually redeemed, signing transactions to withdraw from the bitcoin reserve.

Coincidentally, the main user concerns when using ecash come from its privacy-preserving qualities. Due to there being no account balances, successfully auditing a mint to check its supposed reserves against its liabilities is rather difficult. And since there are no accounts, a trusted custodian must be responsible for holding enough of the reserve asset against the total supply of ecash held by unknown users of the mint. The mint itself is a trusted third party responsible for both appropriate monetary issuance and being able to make depositors whole at time of redemption. This is another prudent parallel to our current banking system, similarly true in both a regional bank and the Federal Reserve itself, of course, with none-to-little of the privacy benefits. These concerns can be theoretically met with clever proof-of-liability schemes such as the one proposed for Cashu by Calle, which publicly generates a monthly token burn list and a monthly token issuance list, rotating issuance keys after every monthly epoch. Both of these lists simply consist of the blind signatures representing their specific ecash denominations from their issuance, and users can check that their own transactions are present in their respective monthly list. The liabilities of the mint are the difference between the mint and the burn list, and thus should be similarly demonstrated within the reserve asset wallet. Proof of reserves is simple with a bitcoin-backed financial service (a public bitcoin wallet), but proof-of-liabilities is significantly more difficult. Concerns of economic debasement and associated custodial risk are nonnegotiable on the base layer of Bitcoin, and yet these real risks are easily mitigated depending on how you use the mint. If a Chaumian mint instance such as Cashu or Fedimint sees user volume at significant scale mostly for extremely short-term payment needs, proper usage of ecash – funding and withdrawing from a busy mint nearly instantaneously – leaves little time for monetary debasement nor reserve asset theft.

Ideal Banking

> "I believe this will be the ultimate fate of Bitcoin, to be the 'high-powered money' that serves as a reserve currency for banks that issue their own digital cash. Most Bitcoin transactions will occur between banks, to settle net transfers. Bitcoin transactions by private individuals will be as rare as... well, as Bitcoin based purchases are today."
>
> Hal Finney

Trust is a necessary component of many of the beneficial financial services employed by the US banking system. This remains true now as well as during the gold window. Loans, fractional reserve banking, and counterparty risk are all possible on a bitcoin standard, much like it was on previous hard money standards. By decentralizing the manipulation of monetary issuance away from central pardoners, Bitcoin has supplanted USTs as the ideal reserve asset for a new banking system. While it is perhaps seen as a failure to simply replace the instrument banks use to settle their reserves with bitcoin, the elimination of these special privileges from the Fed as reserve asset issuers – and the replacement being a disinflationary, censorship-resistant asset – will have profound effects on the current status quo of monetary manipulation. Bitcoin's base layer simply cannot service 8 billion people, but proper tooling in layers can allow this scarce, neutral asset unfettered access to a stable monetary policy – a revolution in banking, financial, and economic reality as we know it. Layer 2s are delegated as such due to their trustless ability to settle back to the mainchain without any third party. But ecash enables an entirely new interoperability between Layer 2s and traditional financial services, with an innate ability to be created specifically and timely in accordance with customer demands and needs. Behind every online community that warrants certain privacy needs for their users could be another unique interaction of Cashu. In order to distribute mining rewards privately, mining pool operators can use tools such as FediPools to maximize anonymity sets derived from mining reward payments.

The future of banking is not stablecoin issuers providing opportunities for the global south to buy US debt; the future is every website, every digital community, threatening to run their own ecash instance, backed by bitcoin, the only neutral reserve asset, when their current financial counterparties are eventually cut off. David Chaum built the tooling and constructed the ideas needed for everyone to be their own bank in the 1980s, and yet those were the days of double-digit interest rates and the largest onshoring of dollar demand in the modern economic era. Now, as the US banking system is showing serious fundamental cracks – from UST markets marking unrealized duration risk losses to increasing depositor centralization in the Big Four American banks to literal government seizure of some of the largest regional banks in the country – it is no surprise that a second wave to the ecash revolution has begun.

)(

⋆ SIX ⋆

The Nashian Orientation

> "Now the possible area for evolution is that if, say, an inflation rate of between 1% and 3% is now considered desirable and appropriate in Sweden, then, if it is really controllable, why shouldn't a rate between 1/2 % and 3/2 % be even more desirable?"
>
> John Forbes Nash, Jr.

On June 13, 1928, John Forbes Nash, Jr. was born in Bluefield, West Virginia. The son of an electrical engineer and a school teacher, Nash went on to reinvent the application of mathematics to the field of game theory. While not considered a prolific author, Nash published fifteen papers, with five focusing primarily on the work started by fellow Princeton associates John von Neumann and

Oskar Morgenstern from their 1944 publication *Theory of Games and Economic Behavior.* The premise of their paper was to combine theories of mathematics and economics in order to better understand the strategy and behavior present in a myriad of social organizations. Nash's first paper, *The Bargaining Problem* (1950), would set the axioms he would theorize and advance for the remainder of his life. The paper focused on the problem of exchange between two parties with unique anticipations and rationalities. Even as a first-year graduate student, Nash understood that a common medium of exchange, money, would significantly help narrow the bands of expected positive outcomes between the two peers engaged in bargaining. This simple but profound concept would be extrapolated within his successive papers, breaking open the plane of the bargaining problem from non-zero sum, two-person games into non-cooperative, n-person games by introducing the concept of equilibrium points, coalitions, and behavior patterns. Nash's concept of an equilibrium point in non-cooperative games, in which there is no practical advantage outside of acting within the known common behavior or general strategy within a field or game came to be known as the Nash equilibrium. The field of game theory was forever changed, and the effects from these papers are still of utmost importance in the discussion of political, economic, medicinal and general social fields today.

The concept of a futile coalition against dominant players within non-cooperative games allowed Nash to foresee an economic disadvantage amongst the majority of participants in systems of money with an uneven distribution of legislative administrative capabilities. An allegiance between two effectively powerless agents is inconsequential to the sum of available payoffs in a game. These theoretical assumptions of ineffective cooperation are present all throughout the history of the US dollar system, as coalitions of nations and individuals alike have suffered under financial oppression at the behest of inflation targeting and selective money creation from the reserve currency of the world. The levers of the Federal Reserve acting as the stewards of credit expansion and the pardoners of selective debt growth have empowered the central bank beyond the vulnerabilities of a fair economic system. When the unit of account of the medium of exchange within a bargaining problem is at the whim of subjective central bank targeting, the clarity of the cause of the price signal from the market is distorted at the behest of a select few. If the price of a good increases within a fiat system, is the change in cost due to an increase in demand for the underlying good or a decrease in the demand for the underlying currency? When monetary supply is capable of contraction and expansion due to banker intervention, the signal of cause and effect within the exchange has been distorted beyond any meaningful measure. If the monetary supply was predictable and ensured by a trustless third-party, the monetization and pricing of goods and services would once again be expected to correlate as a function of their supply and demand in distinction from social intervention in the total money supply of the currency used as the medium of exchange.

Honesty within the predictability of monetary policy is key to establishing an equilibrium point in the non-cooperative game that is the modern global economic system. The main issues within the dollar system are those of trust, specifically within the buyer and seller of last resort black box known as the Fed. No matter how much care is taken when drafting up legislation to protect consumers or investing in social systems or infrastructure, the entire balance of the natural boom and bust within an economy is made imperfect at the leisure of the incentives of select, empowered agents with capital control. Interest rates and bond issuance are the two main levers by which these actors manipulate the simulation of a competitive economy on the global stage. Money, a technological tool, has become nothing but a political plaything upsetting the natural order of a competitive economy and perverting the capability of fair pricing of the unit of the account, and thus equal footing for players within an exchange.

Shortly after his groundbreaking graduate study work at Princeton, Nash was hired by the RAND corporation to come out to Santa Monica, CA and help model probabilistic outcomes within the newly-found relationships between nation-states after the sudden crossing into nuclear warfare at the end of World War II. In 1954, Nash, with funding and support by RAND, published a lesser-known paper titled *Parallel Control*, in which he theorized distributed systems and parallel computation well before the introduction of the personal computer or even the widespread saturation of the television into the American home. In a since-published letter to the NSA, Nash came to the mathematical conclusion that encryption would always outpace decryption, as the incentives for the needed computation of wanted encryption would exponentially grow versus the linear demands of functional decryption. The bounds and axioms of the discovered incentive functions going back to *The Bargaining Problem* would continue to mature through the decade within Nash's work. Toward the end of the 1960s and well into the early 1990s, Nash's research suffered greatly from his schizophrenia. Despite these lost years, the parameters and revelations within his work came to a tangible head when Nixon severed the dollar from gold at the beginning of the 1970s and the US economy swiftly experienced periods of continued high inflation throughout the decade.

Those closest to Nash attribute the awarding of the 1994 Nobel Prize in Economics for recognition of his work in game theory as a pivotal moment within his relationship with his illness. Despite not being allowed to give the traditional lecture after the ceremony, this long overdue celebration of his landmark papers written nearly 40 years ago gifted Nash the clarity or social confidence to once again publicly resume teaching and researching within academia. The end of the 1990s brought Nash back to work on an economic idea from decades prior that had caused him to flee to Europe at the time in hopes of stronger monetary policy – and perhaps his most important paper and evolving lecture, *Ideal Money*. Having seen his fears come to life with the debasement of purchasing power of the US dollar due to central banking manipulation, Nash spent the remainder of his life considering a true paradigm shift to monetary policy and the dichotomy of currency and commodity within the global non-cooperative game of macroeconomics.

> "Our proposal is that a preferable version of a general system for the transferring of utility, thus a 'medium of exchange', would be structured so as to provide a medium with a natural (and reliable!) stability of value. And this stability of value would be particularly of benefit in connection with contracts or exchanges involving long time periods for the complete performance of the contract or exchange."
> John Forbes Nash, Jr.

Ideal money is defined as one "intrinsically free of inflation." This brings up the necessity of clarity upon which definition of "inflation" is meant within the context Nash is referring to. There is both monetary inflation, an increase in units of currency, as well as price inflation, an increase in the costs of goods and services; the US Treasury and the Federal Reserve react with monetary policy relative to price inflation data found in CPI, the Consumer Price Index. Ideal money, if properly actualized, would take the place of these arbitrary indexes used currently for inflation targeting by central banks, and eventually become the politically-neutral unit of global economic activity. If N is the ideal targeted inflation rate, surely N/2 would be better. Understanding the incentives of arbitrary inflation targeting by select players were too perverse to be left uncapitalized on, Nash suggested the ideal rate to be zero.

> "Our observation, based on thinking in terms of 'the long term' rather than in terms of 'short range expediency,' was simply that there is no ideal rate of inflation that should be selected and chosen as the target but rather that the ideal concept would necessarily be that of a zero rate for what is called inflation."
> John Forbes Nash, Jr.

Instead of targeting 2% price inflation relative to a CPI-like index, a central bank could achieve an exchange stability of 0% via relative monetary policy. To achieve this, an increase in the price of an ideal money would be met with a decrease in monetary inflation, or the number of circulating units of the fiat pair. Conversely, if this ideal money lost purchasing power, central banks would trigger a reactive issuance of monetary units. A "zero rate for what is called inflation" does not imply zero monetary issuance, but rather sets the ideal target of zero relative to volatility in exchange stability.

> "What inflation targeting does is to open up the possibility that somehow the various major currencies may evolve to develop stability of value. And in this sense there could be 'asymptotically ideal money' in that an evolving trend could lead to the value stability that would constitute a major improvement in quality."
> John Forbes Nash, Jr.

Bitcoin, much like gold and oil, currently does have monetary inflation, as more units are added with every found block. Unlike gold or oil however, over 90% of the total supply of bitcoin has already been issued, and as each block is found, bitcoin appears to asymptotically approach zero monetary inflation. It does, however, eventually transition from disinflationary to deflationary, reaching zero monetary inflation after 32 halvings. However, an issuance of money completely free of monetary inflation would incentivize hoarding, leading to an uncirculated money exploitable to those closest to its issuance. This was referred to as "safe-deposit box singularity," and its solution was presented by Nash within his concept of an asymptotic money supply targeting. Complete with user error leading to lost coins, Bitcoin will almost certainly achieve sub-zero monetary inflation. Seeing as how this is not a true asymptote, clearly this cannot be the axiom nor definition of inflation Nash was referring to. The true asymptotic approach to zero inflation occurs over time within the long-term exchange of a unit with a weak economic policy for a unit with a stronger economic policy. As bitcoin continues to see cost increase relative to the dollar, the dollar thus approaches, but never quite reaches zero price inflation.

Whether Nash was specifically behind the Satoshi Nakamoto pseudonym is certainly up for debate, but Bitcoin's disinflationary issuance policy, with its asymptotic approach to zero inflation, is the conceptual actualization of his *Ideal Money*. Not only does Bitcoin solve the issues of arbitrary inflation targeting, but it also does so by establishing an equilibrium within the incentive model of the system by removing centralizing factors in consensus control.

> "But a modern alternative is possible, one that would provide a good standard independent of state pardoners. This idea occurred to me comparatively recently. But the possibilities with regard to actually establishing a norm of money systems which could qualify as of "ideal" type are dependent on the political circumstances of the world. If the world had in fact become a single empire with a central government for the whole world, then what is now international trade, with shipping on the oceans through areas considered to be the property of no state, would be replaced by the equivalent of domestic commerce within the USA. And this would profoundly modify the circumstances relevant to the establishing of "good" or "bad" systems of money."
> John Forbes Nash, Jr.

The main advantage of Bitcoin is the removal of those levers of expansion and contraction from the dominant coalition of central bankers and places the predictability of policy and validation of settlement for a universal unit of account within the hands of every willing participant within the system. By utilizing the revelations within Nash's found axioms of game theory within the grand bargaining problem of a modern economy, Bitcoin disarms the power structures and coalitions formed around monetary control and creation.

> "What I have to suggest is not viewed as appropriate for the world empire context."
>
> John Forbes Nash, Jr.

PART TWO
THE FIGHT FOR BITCOIN

⟞ Seven ⟝

Water's Warm Maximalism

"Everybody trying to PvP when the
game is PvE."
Edward Snowden

The revolution will not be centralized. The ideal peaceful revolution that Bitcoin could be will not enable solely one class, one ideology or one political party to replace themselves as the new king of the hill. If Bitcoin's social consensus is commandeered by one homogeneous group, the necessary ideal of decentralization has failed.

Bitcoin's governance is upheld by both social and economic nodes, and this political structure is far from the traditional democracy often misrepresented by both the many critics and proponents of

Bitcoin alike. Bitcoin is not a democracy in which every node is an equal vote, and that is for a good reason in the ever-unfolding socio-economic game theory presented by the protocol. Those with skin in the game, in the form of network wealth in satoshis as well as Bitcoin-specific hardware such as ASICs, have more incentives to ossify and protect the economic policy of the Bitcoin network than a nocoiner or someone relatively new to the system.

This is by design. Rather than giving unelected Cantillonaires power to take advantage of proximity to the money printer, which is the current incentive of our fiat system, this new structure allows all sorts of participants from all sorts of socio-economic positions a fair shot at using a system with a predictable governance; this is the only way to achieve true equity. That is perhaps a controversial opinion, but there is simply no fair way to distribute funds or tokens of economic activity across an ever-changing and dynamic population. Thus the only way to achieve equity is by supplying everyone with an equal opportunity to utilize a predictable economic governance system with no centralized, trusted mediators and no large stakeholders lording threats of difficulty bombs to enforce consensus changes over the masses. The irony of the social adoption of proof-of-stake systems in the traditional progressive political class due to misunderstood environmental metrics is that hypocritical recreating of the many problems of the legacy system with a technological bastardization of the Nakamoto Consensus, leading to compounding governance from venture capitalists and other beneficiaries of these pre-mined tokens.

Equity does not mean trusted third parties take a snapshot of the world and hand out equal amounts of tokens and wish you luck; equity means every participant in the network has an equal and predictable opportunity to utilize a financial network that promotes savings. Rather than a leaking entropic force such as inflation debasing your capital, every payment you receive gains in relative economic value as the available supply issuance decreases in half every four years. This idea of "water's warm" maximalism is not to shriek and yell loudly when a potentially misinformed voice says something that goes against the incentive structures of the one-of-a-kind Bitcoin network, but rather to meet their misrepresentations with facts and kindness. Screaming that the 70% or more pre-mine of a network innately makes it a scam is not doing anyone any good, despite it being a fair piece of evidence that perhaps the incentives and intentions of the founders of said Cantillonaire coins are not aligned with these greater concepts of equity and opportunity. The Bitcoin network is both represented by members that will fight tooth and nail for the sovereign individual, understanding that an empowered individual breeds an empowered collective, as well as traditionally progressive voices that fight for a fairer network for the collective, understanding that a better society will lead to happier and healthier individuals.

These concepts are not at all in contrast with each other and in fact are completely aligned toward the greater good of the human condition, which contains both the individual experience as well as the group consensus of the greater species. Lately, much division and discord have been sewn on social media platforms between these two ideologies as if the war is to be fought among the parties of the working class and not as a united effort against the bigger forces of enslavement, control and authoritarian entities that make up the many faces of the seen and unseen ruling class. The cheap and lazy dismissal of Bitcoin Maximalism as a close-minded ideology has to be fought not with potentially concept-confirming ad hominem attacks but with focused and kind rebuttals built upon understanding, grokking, and even self-reflective critical skepticism on our own beloved protocol.

Bitcoin simply must be for enemies, or it will never be for friends. And the way we strengthen the capability of the network is not by trying to fruitlessly excommunicate others from access to the knowledge needed to become a strong economic and social node but rather by providing careful, articulate arguments to persuade even the most polar opposite of philosophies we have been trained and influenced to reject. Many in the Bitcoin space have found themselves politically homeless, with a strong distrust of the government and the large incumbent power structures that have misled us into vile hatred directed upon foreign populations we have never even interacted with. This top-down propaganda is easy to see for some of us, and yet far too many of us continue on similar actionable attempts of removal for those on the other side of this imaginary aisle. Bitcoiners fighting for sustainable energy sources in the ever-expanding mining industry have simply no governance power over those who believe in order to sustain humanity we need to utilize fossil fuels. This is a good and very powerful concept that truly separates Bitcoin from the other attempts of digital economies, either valiantly tried before Satoshi or fruitlessly attempted after. Those that believe Bitcoin will save the collective spirit of humanity have no governing advantage to those that believe Bitcoin will create a never-before-seen actualization of the sovereign individual. But the bigger point to glean from all of this is not to further distinguish the differences between these parties but rather to illuminate the common ground and the necessity to punch up and not sideways – or even worse, down.

The 2020s arguably have started off with many worrying trends for the health of both the collective and the individual, and frankly both sides will simply need to fight together to protect the only chance that may ever present itself to take the power back from the few and give it to the many; be it many empowered individuals, or the many that make up a strong and healthy collective.

Bitcoin to some is an innately apolitical technology, but the implications on the political and social structures of the planet are massive and continually ever-presenting. The trick in this fight is not to blindly accept any and all proposals by everyone as if everyone is a good actor, but rather to encourage everyone to become a strong economic node to uphold the game theory incentives of the ideal money that is Bitcoin, regardless of their personal intentions of use. We should all be so lucky to see the authoritarian leaders of the planet adopt Bitcoin for their citizens, as long as it is done in a way that brings strength to the network and not bad faith actors attempting to chip away at the few potential attack vectors still present in the system.

We need tangible policy that encourages education, self-custody, and privacy-focused scaling solutions that enable self-sovereignty and not a dystopic co-opting of an open ledger technology that allows further surveillance state actualization against the rights of their people. These concepts will be addressed at length below, but the proper utilization of Satoshi's technological achievement alongside a social movement of kindness and understanding will give us not only the largest number of economic nodes but stronger and self-perpetuating actors capable of prudently expanding the number of network participants that truly understand the necessity of upholding the Bitcoin protocol. Bitcoin is only as strong as its users, and unfortunately the fiery passion of many in our midst gets misconstrued and manipulated by ignorant or bad faith actors to dissuade newcomers from joining the network with the best incentive structures. This is not to say we should censor our voices or pocket our passion, but rather to focus it on lassoing and protecting newcomers from blindly becoming exit liquidity for the foundations responsible for these pre-mined networks that only offer solutions to artificially recreated problems, as well as for centralized, permissioned networks with a total addressable market far below the eventual scope of the Bitcoin network.

At the end of the day, the more people properly educated, the stronger and more robust the network will be; just having a handful of new participants that simply leave their coins on hypothecating, centralized exchanges with zero understanding of the ins and outs of the network does little to further the fight against the forces that have controlled our money and thus our human capital for centuries. In fact, in many cases, it actually hurts the cause of hyperbitcoinization, both by creating opportunities for newcomers to get wrecked by market volatility as well as creating seizable capital for bad faith actors operating exchanges, yield generators, or margin brokers.

There are countless technical and social reasons why many of these altcoin platforms are simply not competing in the same field as Bitcoin, and thus inquiries should be met with sound logic and appropriate reason and tone. Some people are just jerks and should not be platformed or engaged in good faith if so, but for many it is simply a case of ignorance or naivety. Altcoiners are in all likelihood much better candidates for creating strong Bitcoin network economic nodes because they understand many of the concepts behind why Bitcoin matters. They have often simply misplaced them due to coercion from bad faith marketing departments and gross misrepresentations of these platforms by those incentivized to do such.

In much the same way a liberal should not try to box out an anarchist capitalist from participating in the network, neither should a Bitcoiner try to discourage an altcoiner from getting their head on straight and add their "close but no cigar" economic activity to the most secure network. Hardly anyone truly understands the top-to-bottom broad implications that a decentralized, scarce bearer asset like bitcoin brings to the world, and every one of us started from a place of zero understanding of this technological achievement when we started our journey. Too many of the loud voices in the Bitcoin space do more preaching than teaching, and thus many of the new nodes on the network, while good faith zealots lack true depth to properly explain some of the many properties that set Bitcoin apart, and instead fall back on isms and catch phrases rather than a humble approach to learning about the nuances of the network. We can all do a better job of both focusing our tone and message, and we should for the sake of arming our new friends with better arguments to take to their battlefields across the world. There is a false understanding that Bitcoin has already won, and while there are many reasons to believe in the long-lasting potential of this network, there are many things we all take for granted that could use a little humility and humble grokking to ensure the hopeful success of Satoshi's protocol. Perhaps none more important is our ability to discuss with and encourage newcomers, be they ideological antonyms or those hypnotized by altcoin promises, in order to maximize our chance at taking the power back from those centralizing forces. There are many moments when we need to stay toxic and vigilant, but mass adoption will arguably take many approaches. Many of us are simply looking for a home after years of systemic abuse. Welcome them to Bitcoin – the water's warm.

₿

⋠ Eight ⋡
Us and Them

"Haven't you heard it's a battle of words …"
Pink Floyd, "Us and Them"

What really makes Bitcoin different? The apex nature of Bitcoin is not without sound reason, but it is important to understand why many of Satoshi's church have such conviction in the hopeful success of such a unique and disruptive technological experiment. There is an ever-deeper cloud of knowledge billowing out of the thousands of nodes strewn across the planet, and just when it seems to coalesce into a complete and whole picture, another layer of incentives, another extrapolation of game theory, another form of legacy and incumbent systemic dematerialization presents itself.

The focus of this chapter is going to be the true demarcation and separation of Bitcoin from its asset class – the unfortunate peers of cryptocurrency and decentralized networks in name only. Like it or not, the altcoin casino of "all bark, no bite" initial coin offerings, jpeg money laundering schemes, and venture capitalist Cantillon yield-bearing smart contract platforms are most likely here to stay for the foreseeable future; there is simply too much economic incentive in charismatic leaders teaming up with marketing teams to sucker fresh meat into playing the role of unsuspecting exit liquidity for the ever-rotating carousel of pre-mines and ghost chains that is the cryptocurrency market at large. So rather than the beautiful blind dismissal that is more than deserved, let us instead equip ourselves with the knowledge to fight back against these predators with logic and logos.

For starters, the Howey Test, while perhaps being "an older law" in the grand scheme of financial technology, is relatively black and white. In the 1946 court case, the defendants, a Florida citrus company under the name Howey in the Hills Service, were selling large plots of their orange groves to mainly out-of-state investors under the premise and assurance that once the plots were planted and propagated, the profits would be guaranteed to break a certain margin. Only thirteen years prior was the establishment of the Securities Act of 1933, and the following year the Securities and Exchange Act of 1934, in which the Supreme Court gave the newly-formed Securities and Exchange Commission, now known colloquially as the SEC, the exclusive rights to regulate the newly-determined financial instrument of a security contract. This case was monumental in that it established precedent for what exactly determines a security contract versus a stock, a bond, a commodity, an asset or a currency. In this case, the Florida businessmen were offering a leaseback agreement, being as they were agriculture men, to non-growers, on their tracts of land with the future promise of harvesting, pooling and marketing the then non-existent citrus in exchange for a cut of the profits. The SEC sued the Florida men for not registering these transactions with them under the claim that these leases were clearly within the jurisdiction of the Securities and Exchange Commission.

Under the now-known Howey Test, a transaction is an investment contract if:
1. It is an investment of money;
2. There is an expectation of profits from the investment;
3. The investment of money is in a common enterprise; and
4. Any profit comes from the efforts of a promoter or third party.

When a potential security contract is being put up to the test, it is within the interest of the creator and marketer of the entity to **not** want to pass the test; passing the Howey Test means your investment contract has been deemed a security and thus under the jurisdiction of the SEC, and thus punishable by fine (or worse) if established without going through the proper channels of approval via regulatory bodies. In the case of Satoshi's open and fair launch of the Bitcoin network, there was of course no submission of approval via these channels, and thus the question remains if Satoshi was in violation of the Securities Act of 1933 and the SEC. One simply has to look at the first quadrant of the Howey Test to know that in zero ways was the establishment of the Bitcoin network in any sort of violation of the act. Participation in the network to mine bitcoin required the cost of the electricity running over the silicon in the CPUs at the time. This investment – available to any and all who downloaded the protocol – was not an investment of money. And perhaps if you did want to use an expanded definition of the term "money," in which there is precedent as such as using broader terms of investment of "assets," then one simply has to look at the second stipulation and see that nowhere within the white paper, nor any official supporting documentation, nor further yet in the code itself is there any marketing material promising an expectation of profits from the investment of the energy used to mine the bitcoin. The SEC would have to prove that the investment of electricity was an investment of money, and that the open-competition mining of bitcoin at launch was somehow a common enterprise between the miners, the exchanges, and the core developers. Have people surrounding the project committed securities fraud?

Of course, but that is very different from the actual mechanism and anonymous entity responsible for the initial launch of the protocol promising as such. Bitcoin is simply not a security; it's a commodity, an asset, or a currency perhaps, but not a security due to the "immaculate conception" of the project's launch. So where does that leave the other projects in the space? Does Ethereum skirt the same labeling as Bitcoin and find itself avoiding passing the Howey Test? In this humble author's opinion, as well as the opinion of the current and 33rd chair of the Security and Exchange Commission Gary Gensler, it does pass the Howey Test. Again, you do **not** want to pass the Howey Test. The initial "initial coin offering" that was the Ethereum ICO from July to August 2014 was organized and presented by Vitalik Buterin, mostly known at the time for being a writer at *Bitcoin Magazine*, with the concepts first described in a white paper in 2013. Right away we can see that it utilized an online public crowd sale, selling the not-yet-released tokens called ether for bitcoin. If we are giving Bitcoin's case the benefit of the doubt for passing unscathed by the first clause of the Howey Test, perhaps we can be considerate and (for the sake of furthering the case) closely consider the investment of bitcoin as a money or an asset.

Of course, many readers would most likely object to that, as would this writer, but it is important to understand the difference between using an electrical debt versus a traded, global digital currency with a per unit price around $564 and a market cap of nearly $8 billion. The case for Ethereum being a security is furthered when looking at the next clause, and in regard to the Ethereum Foundation's many public statements of further price increases and thus profits for all the initial investors. The marketing teams of the foundation have been quoted many times, as well as Vitalik himself, as perpetuating the assurance of market cap expansion via projects and common enterprise materialized by the Foundation and its promoters. Not only that, Joe Lubin, Ethereum co-founder and CEO of ConsenSys, was recorded talking about the ICO saying, "a person can buy unlimited ether with pseudonyms. We may limit the size of a single purchase to make it easier to disguise ... so that nobody is scared. If you are a whale, and plan to invest several million US dollars' worth, then you can do that in multiple identities. We will ask for a form of real-world identity in the form of an email address just so we can make sure that everything works smoothly through the process, but we won't be requiring it. So we can create a pseudonymous email and identity and purchasing."

While certainly shocking to see such brazen language, this is primary evidence of collusion and common enterprise between the token issuers and the investing parties. This is in clear violation of the four terms set by the Howey Test, and thus one could easily make a case that Ethereum, and the many, many similar initial coin offerings that utilize the rails of their system, are in fact securities and pass the Howey Test with flying colors.

But is that what the supposed free speech and free market defenders that make up the Bitcoin community want? Are we suddenly in favor of government overreach and a retail reckoning that will most likely hurt more working-class investors than it will the venture capitalist backers, such as J.P. Morgan, that has already made out handsomely in fiat and bitcoin terms when they helped kickstart this system? This is certainly a personal bias, but perhaps we can stay well within our lanes of free speech proponents to instead take a pragmatic approach to squashing the narratives of Web3 and these smart contract social networks with technical facts to illuminate the eventual failures and shortcomings of these attempts without the need of the regulatory vengeance of Commissioner Gensler. Bitcoin had the fairest launch of any financial system in existence, never mind the numerous actualizations of equity and fair chance; this simply cannot be said about predominantly pre-mined projects like Ethereum and certainly not for entirely pre-mined projects like Ripple's XRP, in which the entirety of the 100 billion tokenized supply was created and distributed in the genesis "block." Ripple is under litigation by the SEC for violating the Securities Act of 1933 from a last-minute subpoena from the former head of the SEC Jay Clayton around Christmas 2020, days before he made his exit from the commission.

But what sets the consensus of a proof-of-stake system, or a Ripple consensus apart from the Nakamoto Consensus' proof-of-work is not such a simple violation of an 80-plus years-old law, but rather a computer science problem lovingly known as the Byzantine Generals' Problem. The crux of the Byzantine Generals' Problem, in a reductive sense, is how to distribute incorruptible and immutable truth via open and public channels. The Ripple consensus at its core relies on simply just trusting other validators in the gossip pool to not censor your transactions and to order and sequence the transactions via utilization of a centralized clock. The proof-of-stake model that Ethereum transitioned to is similarly relying on a trust system, but this time with a stake-based lottery mechanism that randomly distributes consensus control to validators algorithmically depending on how much equity one has in the system. Over time, the compounding yield will give further and further consensus weight to the stakeholders of the system, a problem further exacerbated by the over 70% pre-mine of tokens given to the Ethereum foundation at genesis for starting the protocol. This governing conflict of interest is clearly shown in the ever-changing monetary policy at the whim of Vitalik and his pre-mine enriched founders. The argument of whether or not this was in good or bad faith is simply irrelevant. Bitcoin did not quite solve the Byzantine Generals' Problem per se via proof-of-work, as there are still statistical, albeit nearly impossible, scenarios of governance corruption with bad faith actors taking dominant control of hash rate. However, in a reality-based probabilistic manner, it does it as well as any mechanism one could hope for; the universal, forgetful function of block discovery paired with the largest block height and highest hash rate makes it exceptionally, astronomically unlikely for any mining cartel to ever be incentivized to take a stab at controlling the Bitcoin network as opposed to acting in good faith.

If we all want Bitcoin to exist and its use protected by free speech, we should find ways to distinguish it from its peers without the use of government regulation. And thus, it is on us to act like a decentralized consumer protection team that uses facts and reason to strike down the marketing teams and narratives of these "decentralized in name only" smart contract platforms. If these parties want the right to exist on the free market, then so do we want the right to talk fairly and freely upon the shortcomings of these products without minimization of lazy bucketing via such terms as "maximalists" or "toxic." It should be no surprise the term Bitcoin Maximalism was defined and coined by the creator of a prominent alternative chain. Bitcoin solves a very real problem that humanity faces, while most of these platforms reinvent many of the financial solutions already solved by trusted third parties while being nothing but a permissioned third-party platform themselves. Bitcoin truly is different, and it is more than okay to proudly think that, but best yet to know why.

₿

⇜ Nine ⇝

The Lightning Round

"Metadata absolutely tells you everything about somebody's life. If you have enough metadata you don't really need content."

Former NSA General Counsel Stewart Baker

The Lightning Network is becoming synonymous with the future of Bitcoin, and not without reason. If Bitcoin is going to become an open monetary network that can service the world's economy, it simply is going to need a second-layer protocol for pertinently scaling the sound monetary properties to a global medium of exchange without modulating or sacrificing many of the beloved properties innately found in the immutable base layer of Nakamoto Consensus. While the United States dollar-denominated purchasing power of a single satoshi cannot easily be predicted a decade away, within a relative range, the historic "sat per byte" metric key to valuing the block space fee on a single main chain transaction can show us that if the market cap of bitcoin is to even remotely approach its total addressable market, base layer utilizations are going to eventually price out the average user for daily use transactions. This is not a disaster, nor an unsolvable problem, but if and when the network begins to flex its Metcalfe's potentiality of exponential growth of unique user addresses, the billions of international participants will not be able to make the multiple purchases a day needed to sustain an economy of such scale at a couple megabytes per ten-minute block. Now before this gets turned into some Bcash-sponsored hit piece, it is crucial to understand why the "big block cartel" lost "The Blocksize War" and why the user-activated soft fork, or UASF, was theorized and enacted by the champions of our ticker in the first place; the sound properties of Bitcoin's blockchain are useless with the centralizing incentives of expanding block size pricing out the ability for everyday users to run their own nodes and keep pace with the expanding broadband and hard drive requirements of such implementation. This was not a frivolous decision, nor an easy battle, but as we continually find out in this space, the truth of the principles of ideal money will continue to win out over marginalized or compromised competitors as long as Bitcoin users equip themselves with decentralizing principles met with healthy skepticism and sound discourse over how best to deploy them.

The mass-adoption-ready second-layer scaling solution to the necessary and prudent economic incentives of a small block base layer is looking more and more everyday like the Lightning Network. One of the main assumptions about Lightning is that it is by default simply more private than a main chain transaction by nature of it being an encrypted transaction between two parties, versus an open ledger transaction anyone with a block explorer can see on the blockchain. While in many ways this is true, the assumed default anonymity and private nature of a Lightning transaction is misleading and should be discussed in an intellectually honest manner in order to encourage good practice and solutions in the network's infancy. In order for Lightning to onboard the billions of users of the future, batching solutions for funding channels on the main chain are going to have to be utilized. This has become exceptionally more possibly private and structurally capable due to the multi-signature capabilities now available from the successful soft fork known as Taproot, but with poor unspent transaction management and industry-wide ubiquitous know-your-customer legislation, there are plenty of ways to expose your identity as you open channels. Again, if Bitcoin is to become a cash-like technological monetary network in countries with less favorable financial freedom laws, it is important we do not allow adversarial entities to control or centralize the onramps and routing infrastructures of this scaling solution, be it via third-party custodial solutions or compromised routing nodes and global network flow analysis.

There are many advocates for not using centralized KYC exchanges, as well as prominent promoters of principles of self-custody in the Bitcoin ecosystem, but there is not a lot of discussion in the Lightning Network space about proper techniques for privacy nor healthy discourse about potential centralizing issues that could come to fruition if we keep on this path. In a Lightning transaction, there are two potential adversaries one must account for: global network eavesdroppers and intermediary adversary nodes. A global network eavesdropper is any entity that can see and analyze traffic on the internet. This includes telecommunication and internet service providers, internet exchanges, chain analysis companies, autonomous systems, national intelligence agencies, and groups running deep packet inspection boxes for flow analysis. These types of bad actors can "only" see encrypted traffic between all nodes – metadata such as to, from, path length and time. These are found from synching to network flow and are not capable of seeing actual content of transactions or messages. The second type of noteworthy entity is intermediary adversary nodes which are compromised pieces of the routing path. While they cannot technically see the original sender or final receiver of the payment due to the onion-esque layering of encrypted packets, they can witness the predecessor node, successor node, payment identifiers, payment amounts (sub fees), and time sent. The main issue of compromised anonymity sets comes from a combination of these two attack vectors by an adversarial entity to create a fairly reasonable assumption of possible originating and final payment nodes, as well as the amount sent and how it was routed. Before one can hypothesize potential solutions, it helps to understand how this is done.

The general assumption of anonymity principles on Lightning Network is that, due to the use of onion routing to create data packets, the intermediary does not know the full length of the payment route nor its position in the path. The predecessor may or may not be the originating sender, and the successor may or may not be the final recipient. Hence the aforementioned assumption that unlike a main chain bitcoin transaction, which is recorded on a public ledger, the Lightning Network is a private transaction routed anonymously. But this anonymity is weak due to payment route captures and repeating transactional behavior leading to predecessor attacks. How this works is that in order for all participants to know the length of paths and economic costs of all paths, in order to optimize for the most effective routes, the full graph of the network needs to be always known to all users. These paths are not chosen in an entropic, randomized manner, but again optimized to find the most effective routes determined by shortest path and cheapest cost.

A compromised adversarial routing node that has total viewership of the network graph can see which peers the node sending information is connected to and thus can deduce by probabilistic reduction of possible paths by elimination, factoring in cost and length of routing paths to find out who is and who is not initially propagating the payment. Payments would be hidden by the encryption of the Sphinx protocol, but a corrupted node can trivially observe they are sending a message without having received one previously, with faster propagation leading to more traceable metadata enabling easier end-to-end route tracing. Slower propagation, while worse for transaction speed, actually makes it harder to identify which message corresponds to which route. By eliminating redundant and inefficient propagations and path payments, compromised nodes can determine relatively easily who is or is not a candidate for originating a transaction. The same goes for being the end receiver of a payment; you would not route an inefficient payment through a node unnecessarily, and thus again, you can determine the cheapest, shortest route via analyzing the visible network graph and find who ends the payment route by eliminating the longer, costlier paths from the small set of potential receiving nodes. If an adversary controls two routing nodes in the path, they can determine the full path of the route and know who is originating and receiving the payment, plus the near exact amount of the payment.

Ironically, private channels make this easier, because if the channel is only known by one person, then that has to be the originator because no one else can publicly view it and thus no one else can use it for routing. An adversarial routing node is still able to see nodes having transactional throughput despite a gap in the public graph, ergo demonstrating a private channel and peer exists, and thus can complete and fill in their own analysis of the channel route. The nodes that are "unconnected" are still executing and broadcasting a traffic fingerprint that is consistent with making a payment. Even with better encryption techniques, non-adjacent nodes can still infer they are part of a payment route based on the specific amount sent, and the timing, again, especially if the propagation is fast. At best, this gives plausible deniability, due to the chance of a handful of potential routes if there are more than one shortest and cheapest paths the payment could have taken. Uncertainty over identifying predecessors and successors only works if you have long, random walks for payment routing, and not the general, common use of shortest and cheapest routes.

The likelihood of loads of adversarial nodes being on the network is perhaps trivial, but to ignore an attack vector is naive and dangerous in the grand scheme of Lightning Network's potentiality. In a lecture given by Claudia Diaz at the Lightning Conference in 2019, a few possible options to combat these vectors were given. The ideal is to construct and use an anonymous transport layer giving true unlinkability between anonymous channels. A network like Tor is unfortunately not resistant to global network adversaries, and end-to-end correlation attacks are still quite possible due to neither delaying the timing of relaying messages nor packaging messages to hide metadata. Tor has been notably susceptible to packet counting attacks in the past, and the utilization of dummy traffic to eliminate the attack vector of timing correlations is a potential solution to this tangible issue. Using mixed nets that are packet-based instead of circuit-based, with continuous time mixes and delayed propagation can create predictable latency, which can lead to much larger anonymity sets. Rather than the circuit-based topology we use now, a layered topology with loops of dummy traffic can lead to un-observability properties and anonymity sets in the hundreds or even thousands – much preferred to the handful of plausible routing nodes with the infrastructure utilized now.

This type of infrastructure can support multiple applications beyond the Lightning Network, and by blending packets from user bases of state chains, Chaumian mints, and even VPN or messenger applications in the loops of predictable, homogeneous dummy traffic, an even larger anonymity set can be created which will allow near-impossible routing analysis of payments, including tangible metadata protection when using private channels. In this scenario, a global network adversary could only see there were packets and traffic sent and received by a specific node, but not to who or where they were sent or received.

This structure does have some trade-offs of course, including needing higher bandwidth due to the volume of packets needed for useful dummy traffic and helpful transactional propagation latency. This solves a lot of the issues brought up by global network adversaries, but unfortunately, the problems with adverse intermediaries are harder to solve for; the inherent lack of entropy in Lightning Network routes optimizing for the economic choices of shorter paths and cheaper routing fees when long, random walks are needed for greater anonymity sets. The current implementation of source routing, described above, has many privacy issues that can be solved with eventual utilization of creative techniques like route blinding or rendezvous routing. The clunky block requirements of hash time locked contracts (HTLCs) can be replaced with point time locked contracts (PTLCs), which use Schnorr signatures to not only save block space but increase practical privacy and thus anonymity sets. The Lightning Network is a brilliant protocol, and has a big story yet to play in the development and success of Bitcoin as a human rights achievement, but only by being critical and skeptical of attack vectors can we successfully preserve the necessary privacy features and not hand our ruling class the complete transactional history of the world's population on a silver platter.

⚡

Ten

There Is No Political Solution

The Orange Party

Bitcoin is for everyone. Not only is Bitcoin for everyone, but Bitcoin is also the first financial system that doesn't even require you to be a human to use it. Eventually, inanimate objects, artificial intelligence scripts, self-driving vehicles and non-human intelligence alike will all be able to access the network by simply holding the private keys to a Bitcoin wallet. Deflationists and entrepreneurs are salivating for the economic implications of such an inclusionary system, but this enthusiasm is surprisingly not often shared by the very people you think would fight for such a development in the general access to savings technology: the modern

American left. The anti-monopoly, anti-Wall Street disdain felt during Occupy Wall Street dissipated in the following decade into an old blue party helmed by careerist legislators fabulously enriched by their years of service to the country. Why would Hillary Clinton, a progressive icon and still formidable influence on American politics, come out against this open monetary network and instead instill fear of an emerging threat to the country's reserve currency status? Why would Elizabeth Warren, a self-described enemy of big banks, ask for strict regulatory pressure on a technology bringing banking services to a country where nearly one-quarter of adults are underbanked? Why would the authors of the Green New Deal turn away from the discourse of how an energy technology like Bitcoin could help monetize and finance a more efficient electrical grid, bringing cheaper power to millions of citizens struggling to pay bills against rising inflation? Bitcoin may be an apolitical protocol, incapable of censoring any transaction no matter what slogan or ideology you might slip into an OP_RETURN, but it is going to permanently shape the incentives of the modern American economy, and thus with it the American political system.

If nothing else, the rise of Bitcoin has shone a light on the ink-covered fingers of those closest to the money printer. With each new hemming and hawing from the civil servant-du-jour's undereducated fear-mongering, the American public can quickly suss out those that enact actual, tangible policy along the lines of their campaign promises from those that are just signaling for social media. Bitcoin is money for enemies, and I hope it always stays that way. The net good of having a trustless, decentralized financial system far outweighs the net negatives of any illicit actors utilizing the Bitcoin blockchain. Of course, we could mention the mass volume and bias criminals have toward using the United States dollar, but regardless of any current use case, universal access to a financial base layer should be a fundamental right for all citizens. There is zero part of using Bitcoin in a peer-to-peer fashion that should be regulated outside the protections of the First Amendment and corresponding free speech laws. Bitcoin is speech; a signature, an output address, a miner fee and a change address. When you are setting transaction fees on your key signer/wallet application, you are actually purchasing preferential real estate in sats per byte of ledger space in a block. To enforce strict regulations on Bitcoin transactions between users would be an affront to the fundamentals of human expression and the mathematical linguistic systems we use to demarcate volatility between parties. Luckily for Bitcoin users, shutting down the expression of mathematical signatures in the Information Age gets more and more complicated, and more importantly, more and more costly, by the year. To ban the use of public cryptography would send constitutional lawyers on high alert as well as require draconian firewalling or physical shutdown of our nation's internet service providers. The assumption that it would be harder to ban Bitcoin rather than to heavily regulate the exchanges and corresponding banking system is perhaps a naive one, but one that brings many opportunities to focus our attention on how best to leverage this technology for the betterment of the country and the world.

For many, Bitcoin is the best chance they have at achieving the American Dream. The American Dream is just that – a dream – for the majority of working-class people in our country. It was only a handful of years after the landmark passing of the Civil Rights Act that our elected officials took us off the gold standard and slowly debased our dollar-denominated purchasing power of savings accounts from coast to coast. These Cantillon assets were purchased and hoarded by our ruling class over the last fifty years as the cost of housing, healthcare, childcare, education and whole food have increased. Wealth inequality has skyrocketed as an ever-smaller circle of elites centralize around the main contributors to our nation's Gross Domestic Product; Big Tech, Big Pharma, and, I'll add, "Big Energy." The lobbying weight this corrupt hydra employs over both ends of our current political dichotomy is indisputably disrupting any pro-people political movement in terms of tangible legislation. Much is said in commercials and tweets, but very few promises are kept, and thus there is tangible bipartisan disapproval in the polls. It gets harder and harder to afford to live near economic activity, and as gas prices rise and housing aspirations dissolve into the horizon, Americans are struggling to even humbly actualize their own interpretation of the American Dream.

We have become a seafaring nation of speculators, adrift in the tides of legislation with soggy representation, where state-sponsored lottery programs make the grade but Bitcoin companies get subpoenaed like the catch of the day.

With near-zero interest rates available for savings accounts and inflationary effects disincentivizing hoarding dollar-denominated purchasing power, Americans have been thrust into the speculative world of payment for order flow public books, illiquid ICOs, unregistered security contracts, and a Federal Reserve Board that will do anything in its power to maintain high index prices and a strong real estate market to demonstrate the alleged health of the nation's economy. Incentives are the name of the game, and it is the direct effects of public policy that has led our once mighty industrial economy into student-loan riddled Redditors playing with a year's salary on signatures for a JPEG of a monkey. As the price of a single Bitcoin starts to create distance and outpace the wages for salaried employees, fewer and fewer opportunities materialize for everyday people to gather a claim in the deflationary world. This reality aside, it is still the fairest, most accessible financial system humans have ever designed, and unlike proof-of-stake systems or central banking, Bitcoin's disinflationary, and ultimately deflationary, predictable supply issuance means it would always be spent via social distribution in payments that increase in purchasing power over time. You cannot be "too late" to

Bitcoin, but before the political system in place is spooked just enough into giving Bitcoin a serious look over, perhaps we should be preparing for a strategic co-opting of this movement.

For a few, Bitcoin is a "single issue" voter topic, meaning that a politician's stand on Bitcoin will either gain or cost them a Bitcoiner's vote, regardless of party affiliation. This idea is beautiful in spirit and there are many reasons to strongly believe in the Trojan horse effects of an innate inclusionary system of peer-to-peer commerce, but the reality is all a politician needs to do these days to raise eyebrows is say, "I like Bitcoin!" While some of these figures may truly understand the power of the Bitcoin brand, they may not be available to engage in all the principles the diverse demographics of Bitcoin believers might carry. Purity tests are dangerous, but they can be useful. This is a rare moment when the plebeians truly know more about this new technology than the current ruling class. If handled properly (please stop working on government chain analysis), the working class can formidably vote with our satoshis and guide the conversation of legislation for our children's betterment. Accepting campaign donations in bitcoin is wonderful, but how about legislation that protects the banking opportunities for Bitcoin companies? How about public investment in the open-source development of protocols that make our citizens' lives better? Can the deflationary effects of longer-term price appreciation on a Bitcoin standard disrupt the endowment model and create better rails for investing in our public education and public infrastructure? How can we create an environment for Bitcoin adoption by politicians without Bitcoin co-option? The selected forgetfulness causing a systemic ignorance of financial literacy has set back too many hard-working people, and Bitcoin education must be handled in a public, unbiased way in order to maximize accessibility and minimize monopolies and profiteering. A voter should be open-hearted to the potential for a properly intentioned candidate, but one should be learned and appropriately skeptical of those that seek office with the aid of Bitcoin. The CARES Act, the greatest upward transfer of wealth in our nation's history, was unanimously endorsed by both sides of the aisle, and only now is our economy truly feeling the effects of that bipartisan legislation.

The solution is not to grow bitter but to grow resilient in holding our elected officials accountable for pro-Bitcoin legislation and to actualize infrastructure growth to compete in the Bitcoin mining field as if it is the national security issue that many already see it as. If we expect our leaders to ever cross the aisle for the betterment of the people, the Bitcoin community itself has to come together and offer helpful but necessary education for politicians in order to best represent the protocol and the pro-human effects it can bring to America's current financial situation. The best vote one has in a kleptocracy is the vote of economic activity, and for the moment it seems the voting class has a real opportunity to gain a foothold in the deflationary world. Intergenerational opportunities like this will not present themselves often, and the truly disruptive reorganization to power structures that Bitcoin could bring might just leave our hero with an open shot at the leviathan's neck. The world is at a breaking point with a pandemic response struggling with policy error at the turn of an economic epoch – a game of chicken coming to a head between human rights violations and centralized banker games. As it departs from the shelter of the "then they laugh at you" harbor and embarks into the dark of the "then they fight you" waters, Bitcoin will need all the political help it can get. Bitcoin is a tool for self-empowerment and an open system built on the fundamental premise that people deserve a better money that works for them over time instead of against them. Those same people that Satoshi coded for also deserve a better government and tangible rules in place to make sure the transition to a Bitcoin standard is as frictionless as possible, with little profiteering for the very same and very corrupt folks that put us in this mess in the first place. This is a time for action and not a time for virtue signaling; this is too important to be left in the hands of careless individuals acting on the economic behalf of Big Government. If Bitcoin can truly be the tool that sets the working class free from banking servitude, then the time is now to ask our politicians not what Bitcoin can do for them, but what they can do for Bitcoin.

The Keys To Victory

> "Nothing is built on stone; all is built on sand, but we must build as if the sand were stone."
>
> Jorge Luis Borges

There is no such thing as digital scarcity. Information always yearns to be free, and with the advent of the transistor (and later the microprocessor), the compression of the universe's infinite states has never been more possible. Music, video, jpegs, an Excel sheet, and even this book itself are all being converted into a serpentine chain of ones and zeros, flung across the globe in packets of lights, only to be captured and stored in stasis in the magnets of our laptops and smartphones.

The Bitcoin network, while a rapid departure in implication, is still bound by the laws of thermodynamics and the binary basics of analog computers found in the many switch transistors that make up a microchip. Bitcoiners love to mock the NFT speculators by making many a meme of "right-clicking" and saving the image reference file these digital signatures point to on the smattering of centralized databases utilized in the digital wash trading schemes of today's artistic commodification.

But while these dunks are very often warranted, they are often accompanied with a misallocation of definition to what their own private keys are accomplishing on the Bitcoin network. There simply is no digital scarcity, just an applied probabilistic utilization of proper private key management. There is nothing special about the massively vast, entropically-derived number that designates your keys that cannot also be right-clicked and copied ad infinitum. In fact, it is very often a terrible idea to artificially reduce your seed phrase to only one safe place in case of human error or an act of God removing yourself from access to your private key. There is also nothing unique about your private key that makes it "private" or "scarce" outside of the probabilistic application of cryptography to astronomically large data sets making the chances of some bad faith actor stumbling upon your private key astronomically unlikely, but not impossible. Would it take the computation power beyond the scope of processors known today attached to power sources the size of our galaxy's sun before a single key was brute forced? Seemingly. Would it make more sense economically to apply this energy in good faith toward securing the network? Seemingly. Would the obvious economic focus be toward a single Satoshi-era wallet, effectively acting as a bug bounty for the security of the entire network? Most likely. Does cryptography move exponentially away from said linear brute force, and with an agreed-upon snapshot of the network, could a change in hashing algorithm reapply this probabilistic application of security and scarcity to the Bitcoin ecosystem?

If these hashing algorithms are significantly broken, the last thing anyone will be worried about is Bitcoin when all nuclear codes, military communications and legacy banking systems are suddenly available and corruptible.

So why is this important to understand? Without proper utilization, self-custody and reasonable privacy practice with your private keys and corresponding UTXO set, Bitcoin is just a public, clunky and slow database, a multiplayer sequel to Windows Excel. You might have heard Bitcoin described as a triple-entry accounting system, and all that means is that alongside the typical input (credit) and output (debit) columns, there is a third entry for signatures or receipts for corresponding witness data to ensure claim on these specific expressions of volatility between two specific parties. This on its own is no technological achievement, and it is only when paired with the two other implications of the Nakamoto Consensus that the social constructs of the Bitcoin protocol begin to take form.

For starters, even if we agree digital scarcity is a misnomer, the application of such is pointless without the ability to prevent a double-spend. A double-spend is a financial issue that only comes to be in non-bearer asset applications; if Alice hands Bob a dollar bill, Alice cannot then go and hand that same dollar bill to Charlie. But in the digital realm, when all data can be reduced to a string of bytes, Alice can email a picture of a dollar bill to Bob, then go ahead and email that very same image to Charlie, Donald, and Edgar, with no future implication of running out of that image reference file. The theoretical hard cap on Bitcoin's supply issuance, an asymptotic approach of just under 21 million, is rendered useless without preventing Alice's ability to double-spend her satoshis by sending the same UTXO to Bob and then again to Charlie. This novel economic application comes from creating a distributed timestamp server with an append-only database system via proof-of-work.

Essential to the ability to snuff out the digital double-spend is utilization of a decentralized transactional ordering system that places Alice's initial transaction to Bob before her attempted secondary fraudulent transaction to Charlie on this triple-entry ledger, immutably and chronologically secured by the amend-only qualifier of the Bitcoin blockchain without use of a centralized clock nor trusted third party. This ability to communicate immutable truth through public, peer-to-peer channels is often misrepresented as a solution to the computer science adage known as the Byzantine Generals' Problem. In actuality, much like the misnomer of digital scarcity, Nakamoto Consensus is not a true solution to the problem but rather another probabilistic application that serves as a usable work-around in lieu of a guaranteed execution. A coordinated mining effort to reorganize a Bitcoin transaction is not impossible, albeit as each consequential nonce is hashed into the next block header, the statistical likelihood and corresponding financial incentive to do such plummets to near impossible-but-still-possible unwanted outcomes.

So a Bitcoin transaction can be reduced to an input, an output, and a signature in this aforementioned triple-entry structure, but in reality multiple inputs from multiple UTXOs can make up an input entry, and in fact nearly always are multiple outputs utilized in the forms of a payment receiver address, a miner fee for writing the transaction into the block, and a change output address for the remainder of satoshis from your UTXOs back into control of your private key. You can think of a UTXO as a $100 bill, with $75 going toward the item purchased, $5 going toward sales tax (playing the role of miner fees) and $20 going back to the payer in change, but in a completely different medium from the initial payment mechanism. Say you do not have a single $100 bill in your wallet, since you got paid for two days work at $50 a day, and instead pay with two $50 bills (those two $50 bills playing the role of dual inputs in a Bitcoin transaction). The difference between paying with two $50s in a cash exchange is incredibly minute, and at no extra cost to the merchant, and thus has no common practical implications on the cost of a transaction. Unfortunately in Bitcoin, this is simply not the case, and with every additional input, the necessity of space in the block increases, thus making your transaction more expensive. This in a vacuum perhaps seems innocuous, but after a long period of incentivizing single inputs and thus a single UTXO per transaction to save block space and thus fees, the spender is now left with a bouquet of smaller UTXOs exacerbating the problem of attempting to avoid multiple inputs in future transactions, plus expanding the complete UTXO set of the Bitcoin network. This has vast compounding effects on the future of Bitcoin in regard to scaling via transactional throughput, especially when attempting to onboard billions of users onto second-layer solutions. This also has implications for incentivizing centralization on both hardware requirements for individuals validating the state of the blockchain as well as mining pools being able to practically dole out rewards to individuals securing the chain without using custodial or third-party solutions, potentially rendering the decentralized nature of the pool moot. Any further attempt to increase block size will result in an exponential expansion of the UTXO set, rendering the privilege of validating consensus to a select few, while simply ignoring the throughput constraints of the current protocol will limit the practical usage of the Bitcoin chain to a select few – both of which renders the practical, decentralized application of digital scarcity, well, practically useless.

Does this mean Bitcoin is doomed to failure? Are we not only handing the transactional history of the Bitcoin network to the powers that be on a dish while rendering future application of the network to a small set of wealthy early adopters who can afford to pay the on-chain fees in a hyperbitcoinization scenario? Of course not, and while unregulated optimism can set one up for an Icarus-like, naivety-induced failure, so too can such negative thinking stunt a growing revolution in the crib; without optimism that Bitcoin can win, there would be no incentive to make change to even try. The key to Bitcoin's victory is not to simply ossify and retain the status quo, but to modulate the potentials of network growth with proper utilization of second-layer solutions that encourage self-custody, privacy, and individual empowerment without compromising the revolutionary core values of the base layer to achieve a semblance of pertinent scalability.

Lightning is the furthest along of these solutions, but many issues still persist. A roadblock in achieving a cash-like privacy on the Lightning Network is the necessity of a hot wallet being connected to an internet service provider at all times in order for successful use of receiving and sending payments on the network. By integrating cold wallet interoperability, whether by non-custodial and seamless atomic to submarine swaps or further Lightning maturation with Eltoo (LN-Symmetry) or ANYPREVOUT, the issues of batching funding and closing channels could be mitigated by hiding massive amounts of users' transactions in single-in-appearance Schnoor signatures, diminishing the block size, economic overhead, and time currently necessary for onboarding the world to Bitcoin. There are even possibilities of yet-to-be-popularized non-Lightning networks that are not as reliant on constant utilization of the main chain whenever a user joined or left the network. These state or federated solutions can create cryptographically-secure transfers of UTXOs between users much like the Lightning Network but without needing to ever eventually settle on the base layer, with anonymous users joining and leaving the network at whim. These types of network infrastructures would allow all the necessary scaling potentials of a global monetary network and unlock the medium of exchange properties of Bitcoin without compromising user privacy nor exposing them to the assumed scarce block space and thus expensive on-chain transactions of the future. There is a lot of work left to do for Bitcoin to ensure its success, but the path to victory will not be illuminated with blind optimism to current shortcomings nor crippling negativity to potential applications only possible via collaboration, due process, and eventual decisive action. There is simply no digital scarcity without proper individual application to a group consensus; the only reason there is any value at all in the Bitcoin network is the sheer belief that certain economic principles of monetary policy will remain, and that practical ownership of keys will unlock their usage. Bitcoin needs to remain practically useful for anyone, or it will become practically useless for everyone.

₿

⋞ Eleven ⋟

Space, Energy, and Time

Building Blocks (with Joe Rodgers)

The computers that mine bitcoin are application-specific integrated circuits, or ASICs. ASICs are specially built and can only perform one operation: hashing SHA-256. They can effectively only mine bitcoin. You cannot install a regular computer operating system on them or ask them to perform any other worthwhile computation outside of mining bitcoin. In fact, the ASICs themselves are incapable of even building the blocks nor broadcasting the blocks to the greater Bitcoin network. The bitcoin mining operators are the people or companies that run the ASICs. Mining operators exist at many sizes, from home miners with a single ASIC to industrial-scale miners who operate thousands of ASICs across many locations. Mining operators also do not build blocks; they simply operate ASICs, which mine for blocks fed to them by the nodes of a mining pool operator.

In order to increase revenue flow by improving the probability of mining a successful block, mining operators join bitcoin mining pools, which are organizations that coordinate multiple mining operators' efforts. By participating in a mining pool, mining operators are rewarded for their proportional contribution to the entire pool. In other words, mining operators receive their fair share of revenue based on their ASICs' contribution in doing work to find blocks. Mining pools are ultimately responsible for building the blocks and broadcasting them to the network. Once blocks are broadcast, they are verified by Bitcoin nodes and further propagated among their peers until these newly mined blocks are received by all nodes.

A candidate block is a potential, successive block that a mining pool intends on adding to the blockchain upon finding an appropriate nonce.

All confirmed blocks on the blockchain start as candidate blocks. Blocks can be thought of as containers that hold the data necessary to settle bitcoin transactions. Transactions are selected from a mempool, a list of unconfirmed bitcoin transactions received by your node. Bitcoin transactions are not instantaneous, yet do achieve a high level of settlement finality once confirmed in a block by the nodes on the Bitcoin network. Blocks also have a maximum block size, or block weight, of around 4 MB. Along with a time constraint, this block size limit introduces a market dynamic where transactions with higher fees will be prioritized and included in blocks before those with low transaction fees. The fee market helps restrict censorship by incentivizing the inclusion of all paying transactions. Candidate blocks are constructed by nodes operating mining pools to meet consensus in order to be included in a successive block – specifically the transaction data and all the necessary information composing a valid block header.

There are six pieces of data included in a block header:

4 byte	Version	The Bitcoin Version Number
32 bytes	Previous Block Hash	The previous block header hash
32 bytes	Merkle Root	A hash of the root of the Merkle tree of this block's transactions
4 bytes	Timestamp	The timestamp of the block in UNIX
4 bytes	Difficulty Target	The difficulty target for the block
4 bytes	Nonce	The counter used by miners to generate a valid hash

To mine a block, you take the five other pieces within a block header, add a nonce – a random number – and hash it using the SHA-256 algorithm, outputting a 256-bit or 32-byte number. If that number is lower than the mining target as outlined in the block header, you have met consensus and can add the block to the blockchain. If you do not meet the mining target, you simply pick another nonce and repeat the hash. Modern

ASICs are measured in how many times a second the machine can run a candidate block header with a nonce through SHA-256. With mining pools coordinating the efforts of thousands of mining operators and even more ASICs, mining pools tell mining operator ASICs where in the nonce field to begin hashing in order to prevent ASICs duplicating work. All parties want to increase hashing efficiency as much as possible in order to increase the probability of finding a valid block and decrease the tangible energy cost of running computation. It is important to understand that candidate blocks are fluid. Transactions are constantly being added to the mempool and miners are incentivized to include transactions with higher fees in order to maximize revenue. Miners scan their mempool for higher-fee transactions and rebuild candidate blocks multiple times during the targeted average ten-minute window for finding a block. This means that if a user prioritizes the settlement of a bitcoin transaction, they can include a large fee to ensure a mining pool will include it in the next block. Blockspace demand will always fluctuate with time within these parameters of consensus, creating Bitcoin's dynamic fee market.

The Duck Curve

FIRST LAW OF THERMODYNAMICS – *The law of conservation of energy states that the total energy of an isolated system is constant; energy can be transformed from one form to another, but can be neither created nor destroyed.*

In 2013, CAISO, or the California Independent System Operator, an energy non-profit in charge of overseeing operations for the state's bulk electric power system, lines, and markets, produced a now-infamous chart on the utility-scale use of solar photovoltaic power.

The chart demonstrates the discrepancies between the electrical demand of the largest state economy and the electrical output of available solar energy during the sunny parts of the day. This visualization is lovingly referred to as the "duck curve" because the energy usage data tracks in a line that resembles the curvature of a duck's back, neck, and head.

The duck curve is a single-day snapshot of a Californian spring day, which exacerbates the spread of energy supply from demand due to it being neither hot enough for air-conditioning nor cold enough to necessitate heat. High solar usage materializes a new challenge for energy providers to balance cheap, context-sensitive supply with the actual, human demand represented in the energy grid. Precisely as the sun sets, working folks come home and turn on their lights – an increase in the demand occurs at the same time solar panels stop generating energy.

A now-emerging need for new and advanced storage technology could help minimize these financial risks of over-generation during the day, and allow the ever-cheaper solar energy market to expand its role in the energy mix. Batteries and advanced electrical grid updates are most likely years away, but perhaps this energy, from an economic standpoint, could be converted, capable of traveling vast distances cheaply while retaining nearly all its entropy and thus the monetized capital spent on its production. With an emerging global remittance market for energy that is Bitcoin, this "over-generation" can be monetized and funneled into cost-effective and profitable ventures that spread their deflationary effects to the consumer. The beauty of Bitcoin's proof-of-work governance, token issuance and security model, is its utilization of a truly universal and forgetful function; no matter how much time or energy has been spent attempting to solve the next block, there is still an equal mathematical opportunity for any active participant on the network to succeed.

This is very unlike proof-of-stake systems that rely on a faux-lottery-esque system of momentary authorization based on shares owned to order and validate transactions, and thus any attempts to compare energy usage are unfounded and disingenuous. This works both ways; a miner can theoretically turn on a single ASIC and solve a block in its first attempt while also turning off its ASIC in a matter of seconds, sending the needed energy back to the grid without limiting its potential for finding blocks when demand lowers and energy can once again be spent on mining. Bitcoin becomes a buyer and seller of energy of last resort. To put this in perspective, aluminum processing, historically one of the industries countries with an abundance of energy participate in, costs significantly more in basis costs to turn production off and on again on a whim, due to the human labor, the operation costs of a safe and executing processing plant, and the many basis points of transporting and finding buyers of a physical metal. A Bitcoin miner can turn thousands of ASICs off and on in a matter of minutes without any relative loss of productivity in block discovery.

Bitcoin is the global free market of energy, be it human, solar, gas, nuclear or coal. Bitcoin simply doesn't care if the energy spent producing hashes comes from "renewables," a misnomer that ignores the concepts of the first law of thermodynamics, cheap and bountiful sources like solar, or even the high capacity means of geothermal energy from a volcano. The universal, forgetful function of Bitcoin's proof-of-work is the great equalizer of the energy market, putting to bed the popular but misconstrued environmental, social, and corporate governance (ESG) narratives of the day.

But the concept of cheap energy is anything but a "narrative," and the economic costs of producing hashes will not lead to an overtaking of the energy grid as we see it constructed now, but rather geographic-independent energy sources that monetize formerly-stranded energy into productive outlets for human consumption. From a countrywide perspective, the main problem with cheaply-sourced energy is an old energy grid that prevents distribution over space and time; our transmission lines can only send energy so far efficiently, and our batteries can only prevent entropy leaks for so long.

The Bitcoin network's remittance properties in regard to energy solves both of these dilemmas. From a local perspective, the main problem with cheaply-sourced environmental energy is apparent in the duck curve; the abundance of supply does not directly correlate with the practical human demand.

Ten years ago, solar energy was the most expensive way to develop new energy creation. Since 2011, the cost of solar energy production has dropped nearly 90%, and utility-scale solar arrays are now the cheapest method of building and operating power generation. Wind turbines have also decreased by around 71% during the same time period and natural gas nearly 32% although one could argue that is from the increased usage of fracking and not from industrial efficiency and direct production-based deflationary effects. In contrast, coal has stayed nearly the same in economic cost per watt. For each doubling of solar capacity, a near 20% decline in solar panel pricing has occurred.

With the knowledge that within an average two-hour period, the sun sends enough solar energy to meet the entire energy demands of the Earth in a calendar year, one can see how the emerging solar capacity production industry is set for a large role in our modernized energy grid.

In coal, nearly 40% of the cost of production is simply supplying the literal coal fuel for the plants themselves. There should be little economic surprise to see that in 2019, 72% of total new energy capacity came from these "renewable" sources, nearly tripling since the start of the millennium. In fact, in 2020, these sources surpassed coal for total output in the United States, a far cry from the below 1% metric for wind and solar respectively (as recently as 2007). This is not an attack on coal or the fossil-fueled industry, and in fact we will absolutely need these types of energy to even get to a time and place when we have a chance of modernizing and efficiently monetizing our grid. If the coal and fossil fuel markets are misunderstood in today's narratives, then nuclear energy is even more poorly misrepresented as dirty, dangerous and useless. The advantages of nuclear power are vast and numerous over the many commonly-proposed solutions to the climate crisis narratives of the ESGers. For one, they require far less human maintenance, with refueling only needed on average every 18 to 24 months, in stark contrast to gas and coal capacity due to considerably more refueling and thus structural maintenance. But mostly, it is the large and reliable baseload of power that nuclear provides that sets it above the rest. A single reactor can produce about one gigawatt of electricity, whereas you would need nearly two or three coal plants or three to four wind or solar plants of similar capacity (1 gigawatt) to give the same actualized load to the energy grid. It is important to understand that capacity is very different from tangible electrical production; capacity is the capable power generation over time, whereas generation is the actualized power produced over time.

Nuclear has by far and away the highest capacity factor of any energy source discovered so far at around 92.5%. Geothermal is next at just below 75%, natural gas around 56% with coal and hydropower around 40%. Again, in stark contrast, we see solar production operating at around 25% capacity. So while nuclear has only around 9% of the total capacity of the United States energy grid, it provides nearly 20% of total electrical energy produced and consumed. Nuclear provides maximum power more than 93% of the year and is responsible for a fifth of the country's power production since 1990. The capacity discrepancy between nuclear (92.5%) and solar (25%), the head and tail of our energy grid's production capacity, is where Bitcoin's next use case comes to life. By being a buyer independent of grid demand of last resort for the high-capacity, high-cost output of nuclear, and by being a seller of last resort for the low-capacity, low-cost output of solar, Bitcoin feasts on both the belly and the neck of the duck curve.

Much in the same way Bitcoin fights for financial inclusion and freedom due to its monetary policy and decentralized governance, the remittance energy market of Bitcoin dematerializes the subsidized and monopolistic state-regulated energy systems of the world. State-operated power companies supply power to half of the energy grid of the United States. These investor-owned utilities are guaranteed a certain rate of profits from power plants, so even if actual market costs of sources make operating more expensive, the monopolies are set up in such a way that that is not an attack on their profits. This lock-in effect means we have existing fossil plants that have already been invested into and thus the cost of producing one unit of energy is "cheaper" for said owner-operators rather than investing in new infrastructure that could distribute the deflationary effects of cheap energy around the energy grid and back toward the consumers and purchasers. The incentives of transitioning to cheap energy sources are not exploited for the good of the people due to these power conglomerate monopolies perpetuating an unfree market.

Subsidies from said companies equate to around $31 per megawatt of solar, $26 per megawatt of wind, $28 per megawatt for natural gas, and nearly $41 per megawatt of coal. Much like how we can easily understand the subsidized dollar hot dog of Costco is just as unreliable a metric of inflation as our government-issued Consumer Price Index, we can see how our energy grid is in need of a truly free market to unlock deflationary effects for consumers. For the first time in history, Bitcoin provides that free market to the very real and tangible energy equation of the universe. Within the forgetful, universal function inherent to the Nakamoto Consensus, Bitcoin allows a truly permissionless energy remittance market to effectively and efficiently create the first true, accurate price of energy over both time and space. This containment of entropy within our collective energy systems will have a vast and powerful effect on our individual ability to store spent human energy. With Bitcoin's direct relationship between financial expression via money as a communications tool and the laws of thermodynamics, we will be able to be more efficient and productive as humans, individually and collectively. As Bitcoin dematerializes the incentive structure of the petrodollar and becomes the ultimate unit of account, it leaves behind a wake of broken energy models and doubters in the cryptographically-secure and suddenly-free financial market. This carnage will be replicated in the dissolving of monopolies and power structures of the global energy market. There is simply no energy wasted in the Bitcoin network, much like there is no energy wasted in the universe. Bitcoin might just turn out to be the most important discovery in the monetization of energy in the history of humanity.

The Commodity of Time

> "I'm having a hard time, living the good life, well I know I was losing time . . ."
> The Grateful Dead

There's a lot of talk about time in the Bitcoin space, and for good reason. A fundamental mechanic of the solution to the Byzantine Generals' Problem is the immutability of the timestamp that orders all

Bitcoin transactions. Without this component, the capped supply issuance that ensures digital scarcity would be meaningless; it doesn't matter how little bitcoin exists if one can just double-spend the same UTXO at a whim.

Proof-of-work creates immutable, decentralized truth by necessitating not just energy but also the time spent searching for nonces for output hashes with enough leading zeros to bring the next block header below the current difficulty target. Bitcoin does a brilliant job of utilizing the standardized local clock of a processor on the network to find an average of time spent (600 seconds target per block) across the whole network without relying on a centralized clock source to validate transaction orders. People scoff at Bitcoin transactions being inefficient or slow without realizing the implications of a global, digitally scarce, permissionless bearer asset with an immutable, final settlement in under half an hour. The blockchain is simply a database of transactional signatures crystalized in impunity via a continuous hash string of blockheaders hashed with candidate block transactions in order to find the next blockheader. By stacking the previous blocks output hash on top of a universal forgetful function to find the next nonce, the serpentine ledger chain becomes ever more immutable; as every block stacks alongside the upward difficulty adjustment continuing its decade ascent, it becomes harder, and importantly, more wasteful for a bad faith actor to try and reorganize spends.

The act of spending electrical energy is not enough to find value in the digital space. It must be applied directly to spending time effectively, accurately computing within the consensus and thus securing the Bitcoin blockchain.

The Grateful Dead weren't always known by that name, and in fact, they got their first public audiences performing under the name "The Warlocks." Unbeknown to each other at the time, they shared that name with a young, upstart art band out of New York City. When the slow and lossy communications reached their respective coast via the new, blossoming independent music scene, they both decided to change their name. The Dead went on to see fairly imminent success throughout the following decades, while their counterparts changed their name to The Velvet Underground and enjoyed somewhat critical but overall muted popularity until a resurgence of their canon in the late 70s. Neither one of them wanted to spend the time to make a claim to their brand, and thus both moved on without so much of a hint of any litigation or litigators. The Dead did a lot of things that are unheard of today in the hyper-commodification era of art, but perhaps none more important than allowing technologically-savvy fans to bring their own recording equipment into their venues and tape the improvisation-heavy performances for their own non-commercial use. A devoted taping community grew out of this allowance, and an entirely new way for hungry fans to engage with the product gave rise to a peer-to-peer market of tapes of shows highlighted for a spattering of personal reasons; someone's one-hundredth show, a birthday, New Year's Eve, debut of new material, a particularly good version of a beloved song, etc. Over time, this strictly-non-commercially-incentivized community drove each other to higher heights of recording quality, with new masters, new techniques, better microphones and better gear led to a powerful, decentralized taper community ready to offer their celluloid of choice for yours in a free market of experiences.

An official series of these releases were called Dick's Picks, named after the long-time soundboard engineer of the band who utilized the data harvested from decades of trade and discussion among diehards to find the overwhelming favored shows of interest and, pulling from the archives of recordings directly from the band's own soundboard, released commercial products of high-quality directly targeted at the fans who made those shows famous in the first place by taping and trading their experience. It seemed paradoxical, knowing that nearly every show the band has ever played at this point has been recorded, located, and tagged online, legally, and for free, that these box sets could ever retain their initial selling value. Not only did they retain value, the three-disc sets were listed for sale anywhere from $65-$150, appreciating at least three times in value since the February 1996 release. So not only did they compete with the slightly lower-quality but freely-distributed tapes, they created a supply less than ultimate demand, by printing a limited run. The point here is not whether these discs kept pace with gold from 1996 to 2021, but how they leveraged an open market of experiences to be commodified without innate commercial intent. The band put their advertising and commercial outreach into the hands of those that understood the product the best, resulting in a deeper bond between the perceived value of the experience through the network of audience and the value of a high-fidelity commodity for re-experience. Certain nights, the group consciousness of a tuned-in-but-definitely-dropped-out masses, on the stage and off, came together in just the right way; those were the nights you wanted to play in your van on your four-and-a-half hour drive to the next night's show.

A whole community of trading tapes grew alongside the formidable touring empire of the band's now ubiquitous pop-culture presence. They always sold plenty of tickets, plenty of albums, plenty of t-shirts, and whatever loss of property they seemingly endured by allowing their fans this freedom was more than made up in other revenue streams. But beyond the obvious free marketing, production, and distribution, the band got something far more meaningful; they got a large following of humans to experience their lives listening to the recordings of the group. This open network, completely symbiotic to the band's own commercial success, allowed a mutually perceived experience to be commodified and thus socially valued. The audience grew itself, and soon enough the market demanded less tape hiss and the more balanced highs of the eventually-released official discs.

One of the reasons those that did could even afford to drop out of the working class to abscond upon the concrete ribbons was sounder money. It took a minimum-wage worker less than a shift to afford the $4 ticket, and gas had not yet begun its rise from half a dollar a gallon in 1972 to $1.35 in 1981. It did not take a lot of hours to earn enough for a three-show run, and hundreds of fans modeled lifestyle-supporting revenue streams around the nomadic culture; large craft bazaars would pop up in the parking lots with kitchens, arts, and of course tape exchanges.

For many, the Grateful Dead were more than just a hobby – it was their life and livelihood. The lifestyle required such minimal overhead and the dollar was strong enough that the momentum of the summer of love spilled out into the hopeful halls and amphitheaters across the nation. The purchasing power of your time spent in labor was strong against the cheap price of goods and services; your time was worth something. As we find ourselves in an inflating goods and service market (in part) due to an expanding monetary supply, we find our time being devalued below our ability to keep pace with rising prices. We work more and more and get less and less for it. This is a problem that can be solved (in part) with a technological upgrade to our monetary network. By imbuing our time laboring into a disinflationary and decentralized economic protocol, instead of fighting a compounding, hopeless struggle against the leaking entropy from an inflating dollar system, humans can spend more time making beautiful things for themselves and others. Bitcoin's dollar-denominated purchasing power does not rely on the dollar inflating more than the 2% target per year since the third halving algorithmically brought the relative-to-total supply issuance below 1.8%. Imagine a free, global market represented with a deflationary supply backed by geographically-independent, universally permissionless energy sources spending their time carving a hash string of blocks to communicate immutable transactional history through a network of peer-to-peer participants. There are few use cases for a blockchain that would not be better served with a faster, more centralized database, but the historic ledger of volatility between human energy and capital is certainly at a level of demanding such necessity.

The history of humanity deserves a decentralized, open and yet immutable level of trust. Proof-of-work is not just the first probabilistic answer to the Byzantine General's problem. It is also the first empirically sound answer to communally experienced time, and brings with it the assurance and ability for users to trust the commodity of time that is Bitcoin in the future. Bitcoin does change time preference in a literal time mechanism, for proof-of-work is a proof of history of spent computational power. It is a clock, just not a predictive clock. Mostly useless for accurately planning future events, in actuality it is an immutably true and decentralized standard of history and time – a decentralized time stamp server in order to solve the digital double-spend problem.

In these use cases, you can see the "time preference" variable changing directly alongside the economic incentive of the protocol. But when did this new standard of history go from being simply a shared database amongst cypherpunks to the immutable ledger of truth we all know today? I would argue it happened just before December 2012, as the nodes enforced the first halving upon the miners, just a few weeks before the astrological calendar of the Mayans ended. The implications that a new standard of time could have on human experience are vast. The path of a group society was incredibly modified with the mechanisms and technological advancements that allowed us to have a group consensus on months, days, hours, minutes and others. Through so-called quantum experiments such as the double-slit experiment, humans have in fact been able to see the modulation of wave forms of propelled atoms depending on the standard of time selected in the data harvesting. Perhaps we could recreate the experiment by taking snapshots each time a block is mined to look for demonstrative effects of a new standard of passing time in the observable universe. But regardless of what unknown implications of empirical, decentralized truth may come in the physics world, the way humans interact with time on a Bitcoin standard is quite different to how we currently operate on a fiat standard. One could make enough for a Dead ticket, the gas to get there, and a place to stay with a day of minimum wage work in 1970. This allowed more resources to be spent on capturing the shows in higher fidelity and an abundance of human time to create a prolific culture around the group. The open-source community around Bitcoin makes it better, stronger and more available to serve more humans, but this social construct would not have coalesced around the protocol without the deflationary effects of the commodification of time via Bitcoin. You can save yourself a lot of time by using Bitcoin to save yourself a lot of time.

₿

⸙ Twelve ⸙

Life After Issuance

"Privacy for the Weak, Transparency
for the Powerful"
Julian Assange

The Bitcoin base layer stands alone; an immutable ledger complete with verifiable fidelity through genesis that allows economic equity via open access to an immutable economic policy of predictable supply issuance upheld by a decentralized consensus via open-competition mining known as proof-of-work. In a field of centralized SQL databases with fiat-denominated units of account, Bitcoin remains the only true state change to the trust models and economic policy that currently dominate our society's ability to save, transact, and generate value. Bitcoin is a Swiss army knife protocol; a distributed, trustless ledger capable of being an anchor for concepts such as decentralized identities, with a robust peer-to-peer network of nodes capable of upholding private communication via gossip protocols. Yet at the end of the day, Bitcoin is a one-of-a-kind settlement network made possible with a new type of asset class native to its base layer. Despite the popularized terminology of "a bitcoin," these denominations are colloquially known as satoshis, of which "a bitcoin" is composed of 100,000,000 million units. A satoshi is the atomic unit of the Bitcoin network, and all transaction fees, values, block rewards and subsidies are all eventually denominated in satoshis at the protocol level.

Native bitcoin transactions are priced in satoshis, whether on the base layer or in a second-layer solution such as Lightning. The mechanisms for determining the fee rate for each type of transaction generally incentivizes larger, infrequent payments toward settling on the base layer, with smaller, more consistent payments incentivized toward settling via shared-UTXO models such as Lightning channels. The crux of this economic incentive is hidden within the specific meanings of "larger" and "smaller" in the context of bitcoin payments. For the purpose of a transaction, Bitcoin payments can be sized within two differentiated metrics: byte size and economic value.

A base layer transaction fee is determined entirely by the byte size requirement of the input(s), output(s), and script-type relative to the current blockspace fee market, and entirely independent of the transaction's value in either satoshi- or dollar-denominations. The ultimate market dynamic for Bitcoin is established within relative blockspace demand, which is naturally priced in its native-asset; satoshis per byte. In reductive terms, the user is purchasing ledger space on the Bitcoin settlement network by paying miners within a non-static fee market that determines relative transactional fees via a sat per byte price on a block-by-block basis. This has many implications for how bitcoin transaction fees are ultimately priced and thus further incentivized. A bitcoin user can purchase ledger space within the same block at the exact same rate as another user despite settling magnitudes less of transactional value. A bitcoin user can also purchase ledger space within the same block at a much higher or lower fee rate despite settling an identical amount of transactional value. A bitcoin user can settle identical transactional value at an identical satoshi/byte rate in an identical block as another user and still ultimately pay differing fees depending on the block space needed, determined by the number of inputs and outputs used, and the pay-to-script type. The important market dynamic to glean from all this is that size of transactional value ultimately has no effect on the cost of the transaction fee when settled on the base layer of bitcoin, and rather entirely determined by the transaction's byte size and relative blockspace demand. This will always incentivize high-value payments to be made on the base layer, independent of security models and ultimate settlement finality. Even with robust second-layer solutions that offer cheaper transactional throughput via routing fees and their own dynamic liquidity markets, the incentives of the blockspace fee market will always encourage larger value settlement on bitcoin's baselayer.

Smaller value payments on shared-UTXO models such as Lightning or even federated, Chaumian models such as Fedimint, Cashu or Liquid, will have transactional fees based on a different type of dynamic market that incentivize certain payment types unique from those on the base layer. In Lightning, your payment fee is actually calculated by the size of the value of the transaction relative to the available liquidity within your routing path. The byte size of the transaction is essentially irrelevant within the market of Lightning channels, and no longer are you paying relative to satoshi per byte, but rather transactional fees are set based on the channel liquidity of your peers. If the routing requirements for your transaction are small due to a smaller transactional value, the less temporary liquidity you need to purchase to route your payment, and thus the smaller the transactional fee. In fact, if you are capable of routing the payment entirely through your own available channel liquidity, your transaction would be free to make at no additional cost to yourself. If you are trying to settle a high-value payment on Lightning, you might find yourself paying higher fees to purchase momentary liquidity from routing peers for near-instant throughput than you would have if you simply settled via a base layer transaction. The fear of second-layer solutions somehow removing all economic incentive for base layer settlement are misconstrued when considering the actual market dynamics of shared-UTXO models and their base layer counterparts.

There is a further misunderstanding within the discussions of Bitcoin's security model being tied to transactional fee rate and the move to second-layer solutions occurring simultaneously with block rewards shrinking. This is a common misconception of Bitcoin's market dynamics that can ultimately be reduced to circular logic; if Bitcoin fails, it fails because it failed to properly monetize, not because of an asymptotic disinflationary supply issuance. Bitcoin's success as a settlement network and economic protocol will be determined long before the 33rd and final epoch begins, instead occurring when the average block subsidy is predominantly consisting of fees paid for blockspace rather than the block reward itself. Every 210,000 blocks, the nodes constituting the Bitcoin network halve the satoshi amount in block rewards given by a block found within consensus. This is incorrectly labeled as the sole provider of the security budget that upholds the hashrate integral to the robustness of Bitcoin's proof-of-work model, and thus ultimately Bitcoin's success. The truth is far more nuanced, and yet also quite simple; Bitcoin only fails by not becoming a settlement network. This is far more reliant on the blockspace demand priced in satoshis than it is on USD-denominated block rewards. If Bitcoin comes even close to approaching its total achievable market as a money, as a commodity, or simply as a unique peer-to-peer settlement network complete with an active user base, it will settle enough value to keep the blockspace filled. When people point out the potential for a diminished security budget in 2140 when Bitcoin is targeted to transition from a disinflationary monetary policy to a deflationary one, ask them "compared to what?" There is simply demand for satoshis in order to settle transactions on the baselayer of Bitcoin or there is not. Relative dollar-denominated terms for monetary protocols such as Swift or Ethereum are incomparable and incompatible. But there is an eventual and important revelation within understanding the UTXO model, blockspace demand, and the limitations of the Bitcoin ledger as a settlement network all relative to population growth and eventual user-base size; there are simply not enough available UTXOs for each person on Earth to hold their own.

When Bitcoin achieves a network beyond one billion users, the majority of Bitcoiners will be forced to use second-layer solutions due to the limitations of a closed-cap monetary system and the novel UTXO model versus the traditional account-based fiat systems. A shared-UTXO model, as described above, still allows access to stable monetary policy and still gives users a stake in the statechange of settlement technology that is the Bitcoin network. All shared-UTXO models are still reliant on the monetary policy of the base layer, and any second-layer solution worth its salt will be designed to be cryptographically-secure and non-custodial. The purpose of this understanding is not to speculate on the design or risk trade-offs associated with Lightning and federations but rather realize the nearly predetermined future of Bitcoin post-issuance. Bitcoin in its final form will continue to be a settlement network with a mechanism innate to all settlement networks; liquidity will flow from those with liquidity needs to those without over time. This is crucial to understand as we postulate what changes need and, arguably more importantly, need not be made today. Bitcoin will most likely become the de facto settlement network for central banks and global commerce and thus will most likely continually price out the majority of users' ability to settle transactions in satoshi terms on the base layer as adoption grows. It is near impossible to estimate what the USD-denominated settlement value will be on Bitcoin in one hundred years, but we can at least estimate the lower bounds of satoshi-denominated settlement fees after issuance. If Bitcoin truly does monetize, and a handful of satoshis costs the equivalent of an hour of labor, most users will be priced out of base layer settlement and UTXO custody.

The implications of this are profound and should carry a lot of weight in any protocol update discussions. Bitcoin's maturation into an ideal money means the choices we make today should be to protect the minority rights of the users of tomorrow. By this understanding, perhaps the concept of base layer transparency should be upheld and preserved, despite the seemingly paradoxical nature of that implication. The biggest issues with the dollar system are the many layers of trusted third parties, political policy centralization and transactional obfuscation present in its operation. Bitcoin solves all of these issues if the base layer is left transparent and privacy-enhancing tools are instead left for shared-UTXO models and second-layer solutions. Of course, central banks and powerful entities will still have access to these models, but they will be economically incentivized to settle on the base layer and thus will be forced to purchase liquidity from routing peers or federated partners.

It may seem like this goes against the nature of Bitcoin and its cypherpunk roots. For those that understand how the market dynamics and scaling limitations of Bitcoin as a settlement network will play out over the coming centuries, may the simple concept of privacy for the weak, transparency for the powerful remain a guiding light.

₿

⋄ Conclusion ⋄

A Means To An End

The bitcoin-dollar will most likely operate throughout the remainder of our lives. State-issued money will certainly not go down without a fight. The only way the Bitcoin experiment will succeed is if its participants realize the extended competitive-cooperative game being played by agents with direct access to the levers of state-issued money. The value of the native asset of the settlement network is ultimately upheld by users' actions. This is meant quite literally, such as when the block reward approaches zero, and also by less obvious means.

"Never sell your bitcoin."

You've probably heard that one before. And it isn't a completely unfounded piece of advice; built into the supply-predictable, demand-elastic protocol of Bitcoin is the assumption of increased purchasing power over time. But to what limit should that be followed? Many Bitcoiners have seen their bitcoin holdings relative to their net worth explode upward and sit in waiting to see how the US dollar system reacts to being cornered by compounding debt service. Anyone telling you anything other than "I don't know" is making grand assumptions about what happens next. As comforting as fractals from previous runs can make us feel, Bitcoin finds itself in quite literally uncharted territory.

As Bitcoin putters away and keeps producing blocks, ossifying its immutable incentives every ten minutes, the global economy finds itself sputtering in the whiplash of central banks trying to taper their fiat Ponzi schemes. Citizens around the world are standing up and removing their economic activity from oppressive regimes, and the ability to live nearly entirely on the Bitcoin standard has never been more technologically accessible. Of everything to be learned from the Blocksize Wars, as the working class attempts their own fork from legacy finance, is that the only votes that matter are from economic nodes. Go ahead and fork Bitcoin and run a billion nodes; if no one is using your consensus for economic activity, your governance over a ghost chain means nothing. The suggestion to conserve your satoshis for the long haul, to hold them for the next generation, is the ethical and incentivized economic strategy, but perhaps we should also be employing our means to remove as much personal economic footprint from the fiat system as we can.

The social implications of a base layer of economic activity that is in the hands of no centralized entity give individuals a true choice. We have an opportunity as humans to stop donating our life energy to vampiric agents that feed off the productivity of the working class. The greatest trick the devil ever pulled was normalizing a compounding 2% inflation on our unit of account. The fiat system is at a crux of disbelief on both sides; Modern Monetary theorists trust the Federal Reserve to control the yield curve, and Bitcoiners think they have already won. We are presented with a unique opportunity to leverage our knowledge and means to set up institutions and systemic infrastructure to ensure Bitcoin can flourish in whatever comes next.

It has never been more important to focus on the fundamentals of Bitcoin and how you can take back control of your economic activity and start being the change you want to see. The game is to create not just as many economic nodes as possible on the Bitcoin network, but to create strong, sustainable nodes that can weather short-term unpredictable price action and regulatory uncertainty. This is not a call to sell your bitcoin, but a call to be conscientious about where you place your energy, who you feed with your capital, and how to best prepare yourself for economic unknowns.

"Not your keys, not your coins" is more than just a catchy colloquialism of the space, but an empirical truth in regard to ownership rights of ledger space on the Bitcoin blockchain. If you give your keys to a custodial centralized exchange, or worse to some yield-generating re-hypothecary, you are giving up your user rights to those UTXOs for nothing more than paper promises from, frankly, dubious venture capitalists. There is no such thing as a free lunch, and exchanges offering any short time frame incentive for users to stake their coins are far outpacing their yield expenses by using your liquidity to trade. You incentivize firms to continue this behavior when you utilize these services and give up your rights as a property holder on the blockchain.

By not doing your duty to protect your bitcoin with the entropy of your own private key, you incentivize bad actors to continue sub-ideal economic activity. Bitcoin needs to be held by its users. It needs to be distributed and in custody of the people in order to siphon energy away from the ever-expanding debt bubble of our fiat system. Inevitably, incumbent banking elites will take custody of bitcoin and stablecoins for their users, and offer banking services to the new Bitcoin class. Satoshi himself talked about the need for bitcoin banks and payment processors, but he never mentioned allowing the legacy system to control these rails out of habit from their years of financial terrorism inflicted on the working class.

Hyperbitcoinization will not be pretty. The overwhelming incentives to be a peaceful, good faith actor will ultimately bring a fair playing field to the world, but the transition there should not be assumed to be without a fair amount of turbulence. Millions of people around the world rely on dollar-denominated philanthropy and subsidies to reliably source such fundamental things we so quickly take for granted such as food, clean water, medicine and electricity. It is important to prepare ourselves to best handle this culmination with grace and sound execution. A systemic flipping from a fiat standard to a Bitcoin standard will require a concentrated effort of economic nodes of self-custodial users to maintain the chain and feed the incentive structure that withholds network integrity for the mutual benefit of all.

Economic models only work if you feed it your economic energy. That is true for both the Bitcoin network and the US dollar system. The only way to preserve the collective human spirit is by carrying on with the very reasons we were plopped on this planet: creating art, writing books, exploring spaces, sharing experiences, extending life and helping it along. Onboarding your community and being loving and patient with all those that deserve it is not only just a neighborly gesture, but also directly incentivized in the presumed expansion of economic network effect. The more robust we make the Bitcoin network by educating, by saving, and by using, the better the chance we have to massively disrupt the centralized incumbent elite.

You may get rich along the way, but the intentions of the ideal money principles behind Bitcoin will spread net-beneficial user access and user rights from this disruptive technological advancement in the human energy economy. How do you create a world that encourages and empowers healthy Bitcoiners? Live somewhere you like, that upholds your views, and that you can be proud to participate in. You are an actionable agent for jurisdictional arbitrage, and you can limit spending your satoshis only to where you want to see growth. Build homes, plant seeds, support creators and developers, and give yourself a saturated life you'll be proud of living in alignment with your beliefs. Trust your instincts that brought you to Bitcoin in the first place, for you have put yourself in place to be given a grand gift of opportunity. There has not and will never be a greater transfer of wealth such as this in the history of human economics. The transistor brought us analog logic, as the microprocessor has brought forth further applications of data storage and manipulation, all culminating into the mesh of human intelligence formulated in the world wide web. Applied digital scarcity in a near-infinite universe is a big deal, and you as a Bitcoiner have a unique opportunity to directly affect the ever-important rest of the decade.

If Bitcoin is going to be a peaceful revolution, then put yourself in a position to be at peace, full and sovereign. But best yet to prepare to protect the network in the many small, yet compounding ways you can.

Fix your money, fix your world.

Glossary

Alan Greenspan – the 13th chairman of the Federal Reserve, a position held from 1987 to 2006, as the longest-tenured chairman of the Federal Reserve, Greenspan was initially nominated by the GOP-led Reagan administration, and then renominated by alternating parties by George H.W. Bush, Bill Clinton, and George W. Bush.

ASIC – application-specific integrated circuit, often used to refer to Bitcoin mining hardware that can only be used to compute SHA-256 hashes.

Barack Obama – the 44th President of the United States representing the DNC, a position held from 2009 through January 2017, Obama oversaw the bailouts and financial policy reactions to the Great Financial Crisis at the end of the 2000s.

Ben Bernanke – the 14th chairman of the Federal Reserve, a position held from 2006 to 2014, overseeing the reaction to the Great Financial Crisis at the end of the 2000s, initially nominated by the GOP-led George W. Bush administration, Bernanke was renominated by the DNC-led Obama administration in 2010.

Binance – a digital asset exchange initially headquartered in China and founded by CZ in July 2017.

Bitfinex – a digital asset exchange initially headquartered in the British Virgin Islands by iFinex Inc., the owner of Tether, in 2012.

Bonds – a debt-obligation issued by a corporation (corporate bonds) or a government (Treasury bonds).

Bretton Woods – a system of monetary management established in 1944 guaranteeing conversion of participating international currencies into US dollars to within 1% of fixed parity rates, with the dollar convertible to gold bullion for foreign central banks at $35 per troy ounce.

Cashu – an open-source, nonfederated implementation of ecash based on a variant of Chaumian blinding designed by David Wagner that allows private transactions in-and-out of the Lightning network as well as between peers of the mint.

CBDC – central bank digital currency; a cryptographic asset issued directly by a central bank or government.

Circle – issuers of USD coin or USDC, a popular digital asset issued by Circle, pegged to the value of the US dollar.

Coinbase – a digital asset exchange initially headquartered in San Francisco by founders Brian Armstrong and Fred Ehrsam in June 2012.

CPI – the Consumer Price Index, a basket of goods and services used by the US to calculate price inflation and set monetary policy.

CZ – Changpeng Zhao, the Chinese Canadian co-founder and CEO of Binance.

DAO – a decentralized autonomous organization.

David Chaum – an American cryptographer, computer scientist, and inventor of ecash, also known for his concept of the Chaumian mint.

DNC – Democratic National Committee, an abbreviation for the oldest continuing political party committee in the US, founded in 1848.

Donald Trump – the 45th President of the United States representing the GOP, a position held from 2017 through January 2021, Trump oversaw tax cuts, historically low interest rates, and the initial pandemic response measures.

DXY – a comparative-strength index of the US dollar versus a basket of prominent international currencies.

Fedimint – a federated implementation of David Chaum's Chaumian mint that allows private transactions in-and-out of the Lightning network as well as between peers of the mint.

FTT – a security token issued by FTX infamous for its role in bankrupting the exchange when its value collapsed in November 2022.

FTX – a digital asset exchange headquartered in the Bahamas by SBF in 2019, which eventually filed for Chapter 11 bankruptcy proceedings in November 2022.

George H. W. Bush – the 41st President of the United States, representing the GOP, a position held from 1989 through January 1993, a former US Ambassador to the United Nations and Director of Central Intelligence, Bush oversaw the negotiations of both the North American Free Trade Agreement, or NAFTA, and the return of the reunified Germany to NATO with Gorbachev's approval. Father of George W. Bush.

George W. Bush – the 43rd President of the United States representing the GOP, a position held from 2001 through January 2009, Bush oversaw the Afghanistan and Iraq wars, the 9/11 domestic security response, and the beginning of the bailouts and financial policy reactions to the Great Financial Crisis at the end of the 2000s. Son of George H. W. Bush.

GOP – Grand Old Party, a nickname for the younger of the two prominent US political parties, founded in 1854.

HTLC – hash time lock contracts, a smart contract that allows time-bound transaction terms to be verifiably implemented so that trustless collaborative transaction models such as Lightning channel opens can be actualized.

Janet Yellen – the 15th chairman of the Federal Reserve, a position held from 2014 to 2018, nominated by the DNC-led Obama administration, Yellen currently serves as the 78th US Secretary of the Treasury since 2021.

Jerome Powell – the 16th chairman of the Federal Reserve, a position held since 2018 when the GOP-led executive branch under Trump nominated the former Undersecretary of the Treasury for domestic finance under George H. W. Bush, Powell was renominated by the DNC-led Biden administration in 2021.

John Forbes Nash, Jr. – the Nobel prize-winning mathematician, game theorist, and author most known for his contributions to game theory and his concept of the Nash equilibrium, who lived from 1928 until a fatal car accident in May 2015.

Libra – a proposed evolution of a stablecoin reliant on a peg to a basket of international currencies announced by Facebook in June 2019 but never seeing actualization.

Lightning Network – a second-layer payment network built on top of the Bitcoin protocol that creates shared-UTXO channels allowing for near-instantaneous transactions with potential increases in user privacy.

Liquid – a Bitcoin-sidechain created by Blockstream in 2018, allowing security token issuances and fast, private transactions between federated members.

M1 Monetary Supply – a country's total available liquid supply of currency used as a medium of exchange.

Nodes – computers running software that validate Bitcoin's consensus via block verification, as well as propagate valid transactions between peers on the network.

Paul Volcker – the 12th chairman of the Federal Reserve, a position held from 1979 to 1987, a period highly influenced by double-digit interest rate hikes and the reactionary Plaza Accord in 1985, initially nominated by the DNC-led Carter administration, Volcker was renominated by the GOP-led Reagan administration in 1983.

Proof-of-Stake – a consensus mechanism that distributes temporary consensus validation authority via a lottery system weighted based on units held.

Proof-of-Work – a consensus mechanism that demands participants expend computation effort and associated energy costs to create an open-competition and probabilistic solution to the Byzantine's General problem by openly propagating incorruptible truth in a decentralized network.

PTLC – point time lock contracts, a smart contract that allows time-bound transaction terms to be verifiably implemented, but uses less signature space, thus discounted transactional fees, than HTLCs, but offers extended privacy applications within use of a specific point on Bitcoin's elliptical curve.

SBF – Sam Bankman-Fried, founder and CEO of FTX, as well as co-founder of Alameda Research, both since filed for Chapter 11 bankruptcy in late 2022.

Short-term Interest Rates – also known as the "money market rate" or "treasury bill rate," these are the rates that set yields of short-term borrowing, or the rate at which government paper is issued on the market.

Stablecoin – a digital asset with a transactional value pegged to the relative purchasing power of a non-digital asset, such as the US dollar or gold.

Steve Mnuchin – the 77th US Secretary of the Treasury, a former Goldman Sachs executive and Yale graduate, Mnuchin held this position during the Trump-era tax cuts and the initial pandemic response measures.

T-Bills – a short-term debt-obligation or bond issued by the US Department of Treasury that matures within a year.

Tether – issuers of USDT, a popular digital asset issued by Tether Holdings Limited, pegged to the value of the US dollar.

The Federal Reserve – the central banking system of the United States, founded in 1913 via the Federal Reserve Act, with three main monetary policy objectives: maximizing employment, stabilizing prices, and moderating long-term interest rates.

The Great Financial Crisis – a worldwide financial crisis that started in 2007 with contagion lasting through 2009 that caused massive reactionary institutional bailouts and other defensive monetary policies in order to prevent total collapse of the global financial system.

US Dollar – currency issued by the United States Government with monetary policy under control of the Federal Reserve and the United States Congress.

USDC – a prominent US dollar stablecoin issued by Circle, predominantly ran on Ethereum rails.

USDT – a prominent US dollar stablecoin asset referred to as Tether in relation to the name of its issuing company, predominantly ran on Ethereum and Tron rails.

UTXO – unspent transaction output, the piece of a bitcoin transaction that remains after a transaction that allows a key-holding user to sign over the satoshis contained into a new transaction.

Acknowledgments

Thank you Satoshi Nakamoto.

Thank you *Bitcoin Magazine* – Joe, AB, CK, Rizzo, Mike, Peter, Ellen, DB and Joakim, among others.

Thank you to the Nashians, Jal Toorey and Jon Gulson.

Thank you Bay Area Bitcoiners – Billy, Tommy, Ex-Frog, Sparx, Casey, Erin, Isabel, Diane, Tony and Fox, among others.

Thank you Max and Stacy.

Thank you Rain.

Special thanks to my family, my friends, my teachers, and all their influences – Mom, Dad, John, Jack, Adam, Matt, Parisa, Christopher, Tommy, Pat, Houshi, Shinobi, The Council, Lola, Nifty, and HodlMagoo, among others.

About the Author

Mark Goodwin is an author, journalist, photographer, and the current Editor-in-Chief of *Bitcoin Magazine*. Goodwin has been publicly in the Bitcoin space since 2017, and began writing for *Bitcoin Magazine* in 2021. Originally from Massachusetts, Goodwin has spent the last decade in the Bay Area, and when not at his desk can be found walking his dog or performing in various musical outfits.

Printed in Great Britain
by Amazon